DK EYEWITNESS BOOKS

BUDDHISM

A Buddhist monk's possessions

Statue of the Buddha as a child

Crystal relic case in the shape of a stupa

Ornamental conch shell

Burmese monk collecting alms

Tibetan bell and vajra

Lotus flowers

Ceremonial headdress worn by a Tibetan lama

LAKE FOREST LIBRARY
360 E. Deerpath
Lake Forest, IL 60045
(847) 234-0648

DK EYEWITNESS BOOKS

BUDDHISM

Written by
PHILIP WILKINSON

Photographed by
STEVE TEAGUE

Plaque showing the
Wheel of Law and
two deer

DK Publishing

Chinese reclining
Buddha

Tibetan
prayer
wheel

Tibetan lama
performing
part of a
prostration
sequence

Lion statue
from a temple
entrance in
the UK

Tibetan
prayer beads

Tibetan figure
with prayer wheel
and beads

Statue of
White Tara

Ornate Burmese
alms bowl

DK

LONDON, NEW YORK,
MELBOURNE, MUNICH, AND DELHI

For Bookwork Ltd.
Editor Annabel Blackledge
Art editor Kate Mullins

For Dorling Kindersley Ltd.
Managing editor Linda Esposito
Managing art editor Jane Thomas
US editors Margaret Parrish, Jenny Siklós
Production controller Erica Rosen
Picture researcher Bridget Tily
Picture librarian Sarah Mills
DTP designer Siu Yin Ho
Jacket designer Chris Drew

Consultant
Peggy Morgan

First American Edition, 2003

Published in the United States by
DK Publishing, Inc.
375 Hudson Street
New York, New York 10014

03 04 05 06 07 08 10 9 8 7 6 5 4 3 2 1

Library of Congress Cataloging-in-Publication Data
Wilkinson, Philip.
    Buddhism / Philip Wilkinson;
    photographed by Steve Teague.
            p. cm. — (DK Eyewitness Guides)
    Includes index.
    ISBN 0-7894-9833-2 (HC) — ISBN 0-7894-9834-0 (ALB)
    alk. paper
    1. Buddhism. I. Title. II. Series.

    BQ4012.W54 2003
    294.3—dc21

    2003051656

Color reproduction by
Colourscan, Singapore
Printed and bound in China by Toppan

Discover more at
www.dk.com

Contents

Monk and two novices

Introducing Buddhism

BIRTHPLACE OF BUDDHISM
Many people believe that Buddhism was born when the Buddha preached his first sermon (p. 16) in Sarnath, near Benares (now called Varanasi) in northern India. Buddha's birth in Lumbini (p. 8), his enlightenment in Bodh Gaya, and his death in Kushinagara (p. 10) are also central to the story of Buddhism.

BUDDHISM BEGAN in India in the 5th century BCE (before the common era, the term used by non-Christians for BC). It spread across Asia and is now practiced by people all over the world. Buddhism is not based on belief in a god or gods. It is instead founded on the teachings of its leader, the Buddha, "the enlightened one." The Buddha taught his followers how to conquer suffering and distress and advised them on how to lead their lives. By following his example, Buddhists move closer to the heightened state of awareness, or enlightenment (p. 10), experienced by the Buddha himself.

Yogis meditating in different positions

TRAINING THE MIND
Early Buddhists learned the skill of meditation from ancient Indian traditions, such as yoga. Meditation is a way of training, calming, and purifying the mind. Buddhists often begin meditation by concentrating on their breathing. They hope to go on to reach a deep understanding of the nature of life.

The Buddha is seen in Hinduism as an incarnation of the god Vishnu.

Mahavira statue from Adishwarji Jain temple, Bombay, India

FOLLOW THE LEADERS
When the Buddha was alive, another great religious leader, Mahavira, was attracting many followers. He was the leader of the Jains, who believe that their faith has always existed, but was rediscovered at this time. The popularity of both the Buddha and Mahavira shows that, at this time, India was a melting pot of religious ideas.

Indra pays homage to the Buddha.

The Buddha sits on a throne decorated with lotus flowers.

ADVICE FROM THE GODS
Many people in India at the time of the Buddha were Hindus, and he is often depicted alongside Hindu gods. Brahma, "the Creator," and Indra, "God of Rain and Warfare," are two of the most important Hindu gods. It is said that when the Buddha achieved enlightenment, Brahma and Indra persuaded him to teach others the truths that he had learned. The Buddha knew this would not be easy.

Stone fragment showing the Buddha with Indra and Brahma

PORTRAYING THE BUDDHA

Depictions of the Buddha vary greatly, depending on where they come from and when they were made. But they all succeed in putting across a sense of the high esteem in which he is held. Statues of the Buddha are often golden and large. This stresses the fact that he was an important figure and worthy of reverence.

The Buddha wears a robe with a decorative border.

Modern statue of the Buddha made of gilded plaster

The Buddha's right hand is turned toward the ground in the Earth-witnessing gesture (p. 15).

Modern book containing Buddhist scriptures in Pali

LANGUAGES OF BUDDHISM

The early scriptures were written down in Pali, an Indian language. The sacred language of India in the Buddha's time was Sanskrit, but he encouraged his followers to use local languages and dialects. Buddhist words have two main forms. Pali is the form used in Theravada Buddhism (pp. 20–21) and in this book. Sanskrit, along with Tibetan and Chinese, is used in Mahayana Buddhism (pp. 24–25).

Thai Buddhist novice monk in the meditation position

THE BUDDHA'S FOLLOWING

Today, there are Buddhists all over the world. They come from many different places and traditions. The Buddha was a great teacher. He spent most of his time traveling and preaching with a group of followers. These followers grew in number and became the first Buddhist monks, who continued to spread the faith.

The Buddha's left hand is in his lap in the meditation gesture.

The Buddha's feet are crossed in the lotus position, a posture often used during meditation.

"Completely have I understood what must be understood, though others failed to understand it. That is the reason why I am a buddha."

BUDDHACARITA
The meeting with the mendicant

It is said that the Buddha had webbed toes, rounded ankles, and projecting heels—these are some of the 32 marks of a great man (pp. 14–15).

The life of the Buddha

BABY BUDDHA
Many statues of the young Siddhatta show him pointing one hand to the Earth and the other to Heaven. After his birth, Siddhatta is said to have taken seven steps each to the north, south, east, and west. He then declared that he alone, on the Earth and in Heaven, was worthy to be revered.

THE MAN WHO WAS to become the Buddha was born Siddhatta Gotama during the 5th century BCE, in an area of India that is now part of Nepal. His family was from the upper class and, according to some accounts of his life, Siddhatta's father was the ruler of a tribe called the Shakya. Siddhatta was therefore a prince. He left his privileged background to search for the truth of human existence and to reach a state of enlightenment. He finally became the leader of what is today one of the oldest and most widespread of all world faiths.

SIGNS OF GREATNESS
Accounts of Siddhatta's birth are full of signs predicting he would lead an exceptional life. He was born in a grove among woods near Lumbini when his mother was on her way to visit her family. In some accounts of the birth, the young prince emerged from his mother's side. He was said to be spotlessly clean when he was born and able to walk right away.

"When born, he was so lustrous and steadfast that it appeared as if the young Sun had come down to Earth."

BUDDHACARITA
The birth of the bodhisattva

18th-century Tibetan painting showing the Buddha taking his first steps

8

A SHELTERED LIFE

Soon after Siddhatta was born, a holy man called Asita visited him at his father's palace. Asita predicted that Siddhatta would become either a great prince or a great religious teacher. Siddhatta's father wanted his son to follow in his own footsteps, so he made sure that Siddhatta lived a sheltered life, staying mostly within the royal palace.

The artist has given the palace a Chinese appearance.

18th-century Tibetan picture of Siddhatta in his father's palace

Relatives mourn a dead man.

Siddhatta witnesses death for the first time.

18th-century Tibetan depiction of Siddhatta watching a funeral procession

READY TO RULE

The young prince Siddhatta lived a life of luxury. This 10th-century Chinese painting shows him riding with one of his servants. Siddhatta's father protected him from life's hardships because he didn't want his thoughts to turn toward religion. Siddhatta married a beautiful young woman called Yashodhara, and it seemed that he would become a ruler of his people as his father wished.

SEEING SUFFERING

When Siddhatta did leave the palace, his father ordered all signs of human suffering to be hidden. But one day Siddhatta caught sight of an old man bent double over his walking stick. The next day, he saw a sick man, and the day after that a funeral procession. On the following day, Siddhatta saw a holy man who had reached a state of calm by leaving behind all worldly comforts.

Section of frieze from the Amaravati stupa in southern India

Siddhatta's faithful servant says farewell.

Gods support the hooves of Siddhatta's horse, so that they make no noise as he leaves the palace in secret.

Siddhatta leaves the palace on his horse Kanthaka.

Prince Siddhatta gives up his horse.

GIVING IT ALL AWAY

Siddhatta decided to give up the comforts of the palace, his fine horses and chariots, and his loving wife and newborn son, Rahula. He believed that this was the only way in which he would find out the truth about human suffering and achieve the peace of mind of the holy man he had seen.

Continued on next page

Continued from previous page

Great going forth

Siddhatta "went forth" into the
world to achieve enlightenment.
If he succeeded, he would escape
the cycle of suffering, death, and
rebirth (pp. 16–17) and develop a
new understanding of life and the
universe. Siddhatta's quest was
not quick or easy—he had to try
several different routes before
he finally succeeded.

18th-century
Tibetan depiction
of the Buddha
cutting his hair

WORLDLINESS AND VANITY
Siddhatta prepared for his spiritual
search by giving up everything to
do with his worldly past. He shaved off his
long hair, because in India at that time hair
was thought to be symbolic of vanity.

*Animal-faced
demons surround
Mara.*

*Mara carries a
mace, ready to
attack Siddhatta.*

17th-century
Japanese statue
of the emaciated
Siddhatta

SIDDHATTA'S SEARCH
After studying with different spiritual
teachers, Siddhatta continued his quest
alone. He became an ascetic—someone who
gives up all comforts—sleeping outdoors
and eating only a little food. But this did not
give him the answers he was searching for.

Stone relief
showing a
group of
demons in
Mara's army

MARA'S ARMY
Mara is an embodiment of death and desire.
He attacked Siddhatta with the help of his
beautiful but deceitful daughters and his
army of demons. Siddhatta called on the Earth
Goddess to bear witness to his merit (p. 15),
and Mara and his army ran away in fear.

Chinese depiction of
the Buddha beneath
the Bodhi Tree

THE ENLIGHTENED ONE

Siddhatta meditated under a tree (now known as the Bodhi Tree) at Bodh Gaya in northeast India. After three days and nights, he finally reached enlightenment. He was free from the fear of suffering and from the cycle of death and rebirth. He could truly be called the Buddha, "the enlightened one."

Leaves from a descendant of the first Bodhi Tree

Triptych showing the
Buddha with two of his followers

FIRST FOLLOWERS

After achieving enlightenment, the Buddha meditated alone for several weeks. He then began to teach others, and soon followers such as Sariputta and Moggallana were learning how the Buddha had attained enlightenment. The Buddha had succeeded through neither extreme luxury nor through asceticism, but through following a Middle Way (pp. 18–19).

"His body gave him no trouble, his eyes never closed, and he looked into his own mind. He thought: 'Here I have found freedom.'"

BUDDHACARITA
The enlightenment

The Buddha told his followers to be calm because he was passing on to his final death.

PASSING AWAY

About 45 years after reaching enlightenment, the time came for the Buddha to achieve parinibbana, or pass on to his final death. Scriptures record that he ate some poisoned food. Knowing that it would cause death, he stopped others from eating it. He then lay on his side and meditated until he passed away.

In depictions of his death, the Buddha always rests his head on his right arm.

Animals and demons mourn the death of the Buddha.

Living for buddhahood

HUNDREDS OF STORIES are told to help people understand the Buddha's teachings (pp. 16–19). Many of the tales concern the previous lives of the Buddha, before he was born as Siddhatta Gotama. They are called Jataka stories and form part of the scriptures in the Pali language (pp. 20–21). The stories show the Buddha-to-be reborn (pp. 16–17) in many different forms. In most cases, he carries out a virtuous deed or an act of self-sacrifice, showing his unique character and ensuring that each of his rebirths is a step on the way to buddhahood.

BODHISATTVA BIRD
The Tibetan story "The Buddha's Law Among the Birds" is similar in form to the Jatakas. Bodhisattva Avalokiteshvara (p. 27) turned himself into a cuckoo. After meditating for a year, he taught all the other birds that they should not be satisfied with the endless round of death and rebirth, but should study the teachings of the Buddha.

Ancient Chinese wine pot in the shape of a monkey

Serpents are often portrayed with many heads.

18th-century Burmese elephant chesspiece

BUILDING BRIDGES
"The Monkey King" is a tale about the King of Benares, who went out hunting monkeys. He saw a monkey king stretch his body across a river to make a bridge so his tribe could escape. In the process, the monkey king injured his back and could not escape himself. The King of Benares was so amazed by the monkey's self-sacrifice that he bathed the animal's wounds.

A MOVING TALE
"The White Elephant" is a tale about a fine white elephant who worked for a king. The king noticed that the elephant was sad and asked what was wrong. The elephant explained that he wanted to go back to the forest to care for his old, blind mother. The king was so moved that he let him return to the forest.

SERPENT'S SPIRIT
"The Serpent King" is about a serpent who often left his watery kingdom to fast, or go without food. One day, the serpent was caught by a human king. The serpent showed the king his beautiful underwater home. "Why do you want to leave this place?" asked the king. "Because I want to be reborn as a man and purify my spirit," replied the serpent.

Stone head of a Naga serpent

GREAT SACRIFICE
"The Hungry Tigress" is a tale about the Buddha-to-be in human form. He and one of his followers came across a starving tigress who was about to eat her own cubs. The Buddha-to-be sent away his follower, then offered his own body to the starving animal. Both the tigress and her cubs feasted on his flesh.

Shakra, "King of the Gods," is sitting in the posture of royal ease.

Shakra, "King of the Gods," is sitting in the posture of royal ease.

Emperor Mandhata is surrounded by dancing women.

Limestone depiction of the Mandhata Jataka

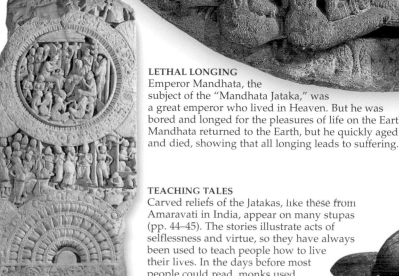

LETHAL LONGING
Emperor Mandhata, the subject of the "Mandhata Jataka," was a great emperor who lived in Heaven. But he was bored and longed for the pleasures of life on the Earth. Mandhata returned to the Earth, but he quickly aged and died, showing that all longing leads to suffering.

TEACHING TALES
Carved reliefs of the Jatakas, like these from Amaravati in India, appear on many stupas (pp. 44–45). The stories illustrate acts of selflessness and virtue, so they have always been used to teach people how to live their lives. In the days before most people could read, monks used the carvings in their lessons.

SELFLESS STAG
"The King and the Deer" is about a king who went hunting. He was going to kill a doe who had a fawn, but a stag stepped forward to offer himself in place of the doe. The king was moved by the stag's bravery and vowed never to kill an animal again.

18th-century wooden statue of a deer from Thailand

13

Features, poses, and gestures

Copy of an early depiction of the Buddha from Burma

LONG BEFORE THE BUDDHA'S time on the Earth, Indian wise men said that there were 32 marks, or features, to be found on a great man. The Buddha had all of these, from the wisdom bump on his head to the wheels on the soles of his feet (p. 43), although not all are shown on every image of him. Each of the 32 features has a special meaning, as do the Buddha's various poses and hand gestures. They represent aspects of his character, and events and activities from his lives.

Copy of the Kamakura Buddha from Japan

FINGERS AND THUMBS
In this gesture, used during meditation, the palms of the hands face upward and the fingers and thumbs touch at the tips. This forms a flattened triangle shape that symbolizes the Three Jewels of Buddhism (p. 18).

The wisdom bump on top of the Buddha's head resembles the turban that was worn by royalty and gods.

The urna between the Buddha's eyes is sometimes called a beauty spot or a wisdom eye.

Burmese Buddha with Mucalinda

SHELTER FROM THE STORM
This statue symbolizes an event in the Buddha's life. The Buddha was meditating during a rainstorm. A cobra called Mucalinda coiled himself around the Buddha and arched his hood over the Buddha's head to form a protective umbrella.

THE FACE OF THE BUDDHA
As depicted here, the Buddha is usually shown with a calm or withdrawn expression and with half-closed eyes, as if he is meditating. This statue also features some of the 32 marks. The Buddha has an urna, or spot, between his eyes and a wisdom bump. He also has elongated ear lobes, which symbolize wisdom and spiritual understanding.

14

The flamelike headdress represents the light of supreme knowledge.

Thai wooden Buddha in the meditating posture

Chinese painted wooden reclining Buddha

Thai bronze Buddha making the Earth-witnessing gesture

DEATH POSTURE
The Buddha is said to have died lying on his side in the reclining posture. The reclining Buddha is often shown wearing monk's robes (pp. 48–49) and resting his head on his right hand, while his left hand is on his hip. His expression is usually serene.

CROSS-LEGGED
When meditating, the Buddha is often shown with his legs crossed in the half-lotus position shown here. This posture had been used for meditation in yoga for many hundreds of years.

WITHOUT WEAPONS
This gesture, with the right hand raised to shoulder height, is common in images of the standing Buddha. It represents fearlessness and also blessing and friendship. It makes clear that the person making the gesture holds no weapon.

CALLING THE EARTH GODDESS
The Earth-witnessing gesture shown here symbolizes the moment in the Buddha's life when he touched the ground during his struggle with Mara. This gesture summoned the Earth Goddess. The Buddha called her to bear witness to the merit, or virtue, he had acquired in his previous lives and the steadfastness with which he withstood Mara's attack.

CALMING THE ELEPHANT
The Buddha is sometimes shown with both hands raised in a gesture of strength and fearlessness. According to one story, the Buddha was once attacked by an angry elephant. The Buddha channeled his great power into this simple gesture and calmed the beast.

"The soles of his feet were marked with wheels ... his fingers and toes were joined by webs ... a circle of soft down grew between his eyebrows ..."

BUDDHACARITA
Asita's visit

Standing Buddha making the gesture of fearlessness and friendship

Buddhist teachings

THE BUDDHA'S MOST important teachings concerned basic truths about existence and advice about how his followers should live. He told people that their lives were part of a repeating cycle of birth, death, and rebirth. The Buddha summed up the problems that most humans have to endure in Four Noble Truths about suffering (pp. 18–19). He then offered a way to overcome suffering through the Noble Eightfold Path. This path allows some people to break free from the cycle of rebirth and achieve the state of enlightenment.

The six realms of rebirth from the Wheel of Life

BORN AGAIN
The endless cycle through the realms of rebirth is known as samsara. Buddhists believe that when a person dies he or she is reborn and a new being is created. This new being could be an animal or even one of the gods. Buddhists do not believe in an essential soul or self, so each reborn being is distinct from the previous life.

Yama, "the Lord of Death," grips the wheel with his teeth.

Heaven, or the realm of the gods, is the highest of the six realms, but it is still only a step on the route to enlightenment.

The realm of the asuras is a place of envy and continuous war.

The scenes around the edge of the wheel illustrate the law of kamma, in which every action depends on other actions.

THE FIRST SERMON
After his enlightenment, the Buddha went to a deer park in Sarnath, near the city of Benares in northern India. He explained to others the truths that had come to him under the Bodhi Tree and told them how they too might reach the state of enlightenment known as nibbana (p. 40).

Copy of a decoration from the roof of the Potala Palace, Lhasa, Tibet

WHEEL OF LAW
The Buddha's sermon in Sarnath became known as "the first turning of the Wheel of Law." The Buddha's teachings are also referred to as the dhamma, which means doctrine, truth, or law. The dhamma sums up the essence of the Buddha's ideas about human suffering and the way to end it.

Hand of the Buddha making the dhamma, or teaching, gesture

WHEEL OF LIFE
Tibetan Buddhists illustrate the cycle of rebirth with the Wheel of Life. The main body of the wheel shows the six realms into which one can be reborn. These are the realms of gods, humans, animals, asuras (warlike demons), hungry spirits, and Hell. Around the edge of the wheel, 12 scenes show how kamma works in human life (p. 40).

Wheel of Life from a Tibetan wall hanging

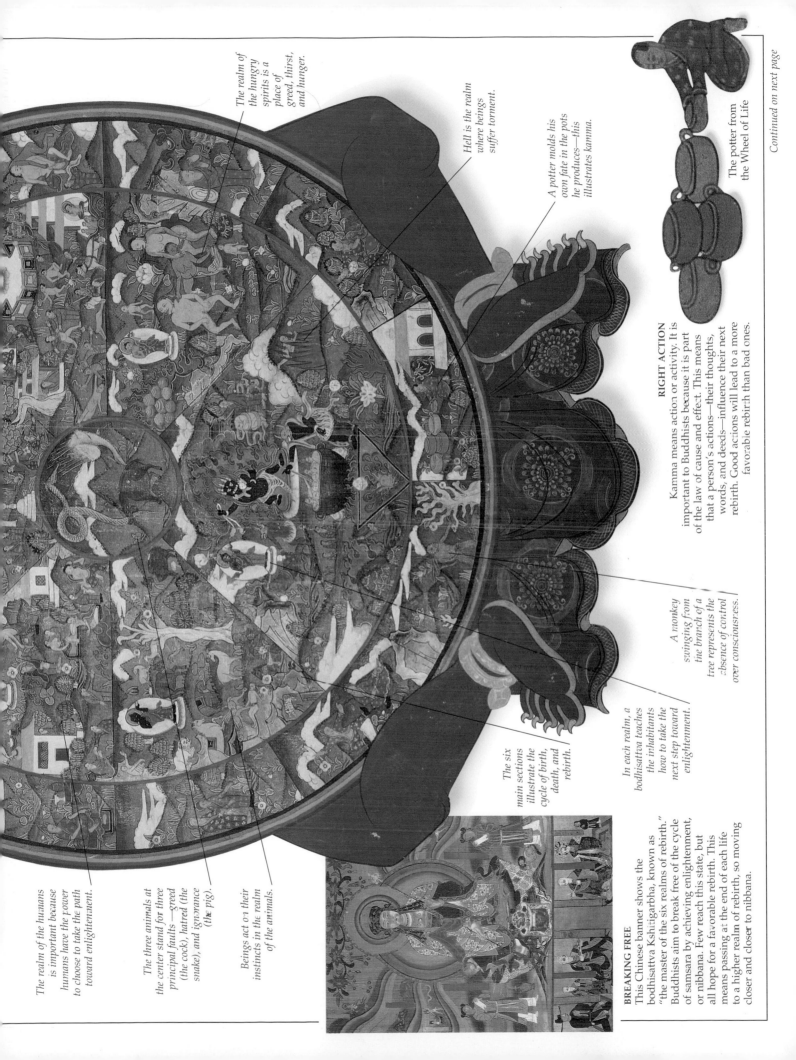

The realm of the hungry spirits is a place of greed, thirst, and hunger.

Hell is the realm where beings suffer torment.

A potter molds his own fate in the pots he produces—this illustrates kamma.

Continued on next page

The potter from the Wheel of Life

RIGHT ACTION
Kamma means action or activity. It is important to Buddhists because it is part of the law of cause and effect. This means that a person's actions—their thoughts, words, and deeds—influence their next rebirth. Good actions will lead to a more favorable rebirth than bad ones.

The realm of the humans is important because humans have the power to choose to take the path toward enlightenment.

The three animals at the center stand for three principal faults—greed (the cock), hatred (the snake), and ignorance (the pig).

Beings act on their instincts in the realm of the animals.

The six main sections illustrate the cycle of birth, death, and rebirth.

In each realm, a bodhisattva teaches the inhabitants how to take the next step toward enlightenment.

A monkey swinging from the branch of a tree represents the absence of control over consciousness.

BREAKING FREE
This Chinese banner shows the bodhisattva Kshitigarbha, known as "the master of the six realms of rebirth." Buddhists aim to break free of the cycle of samsara by achieving enlightenment, or nibbana. Few reach this state, but all hope for a favorable rebirth. This means passing at the end of each life to a higher realm of rebirth, so moving closer and closer to nibbana.

Continued from previous page

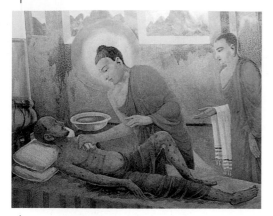

SUFFERING SICKNESS
This painting shows the Buddha helping a monk who is suffering through illness. The Four Noble Truths at the center of the Buddha's teachings are closely linked to human suffering. The Buddha saw that people suffer when they crave things they cannot have. For example, people may crave eternal life, even though everyone has to die.

The Middle Way

There are Four Noble Truths at the center of the Buddha's teachings: all life is suffering, the cause of suffering is craving, the end of suffering comes with release from craving, and the release from suffering comes from following the Noble Eightfold Path. In order to follow the moral guidance of the Noble Eightfold Path, Buddhists must find the balance between luxury and hardship known as the Middle Way. They do not usually wear fancy clothes or rags, instead they dress practically. They do not normally feast or fast, instead they share simple meals.

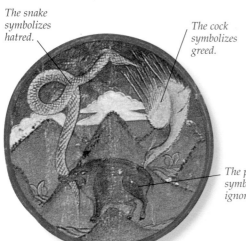

The snake symbolizes hatred.

The cock symbolizes greed.

The pig symbolizes ignorance.

CONSTANT CRAVINGS
The animals in the center of the Wheel of Life symbolize three faults that the Buddha believed people must overcome. These faults are hatred, ignorance, and greed—all of which involve craving. Hatred involves the craving to destroy. Ignorance and greed bring about craving unnecessary things. The three animals chase each other in an endless circle, symbolizing the strong link between the three faults.

INSPIRING TEACHER
This Tibetan mural shows the Buddha teaching the Noble Eightfold Path. The eight parts of this path are right understanding, right intention, right speech, right action, right livelihood, right effort, right mindfulness, and right concentration. The path teaches Buddhists how to overcome greed, hatred, and ignorance, which lead to suffering.

Carved figures embracing, from Borobudur stupa in Java

CONSEQUENCES OF CRAVING
These figures are wrapped up in the world of desire and craving and are ignoring the Noble Eightfold Path. Buddhists believe that it is important to find release from craving because craving leads to moral faults. These faults can, in turn, bring about a poor rebirth.

The eye is drawn upward to the eight discs that decorate the spire.

Thai novice monk caring for a kitten

THE RIGHT JOB
Doi Suthep-Doi forest in Thailand is protected and cared for by Buddhist monks. Buddhists try to observe the Noble Eightfold Path in their livelihood, or work, just as they do in the rest of their lives. They avoid jobs that involve causing suffering to others, such as working as a butcher or trading in arms, and try to do work that benefits other living things. This is known as right livelihood.

This model stupa may once have contained relics of the Buddha.

Teardrop-shaped gems representing the Precious Jewels

PEACE AND HARMONY
The Buddha said that people should behave in a caring way toward other living things to encourage harmony in the world. This is known as right action. He taught people not to harm or kill other beings and not to steal. Early Buddhists reinforced this advice with Five Moral Precepts. These are to avoid harming others, stealing, sexual misconduct, lying, and taking drugs and alcohol.

LITTLE GEMS
The Buddha described three things, or Three Precious Jewels, for Buddhists to turn to when trying to follow the Noble Eightfold Path. They are the Buddha himself, his dhamma, or teachings, and the monastic community known as the sangha (pp. 48–51). Buddhists remember the Three Precious Jewels, which are often represented by three gems, every time they take the Triple Refuge (pp. 54–55).

Images of the Buddha decorate the model.

EIGHTS EVERYWHERE
The qualities of the Noble Eightfold Path are often represented on stupa spires by a series of eight discs. The Wheel of Law has eight spokes and the stupa in Borobudur is made up of eight levels. This repeated use of the number eight reminds Buddhists of the importance of the Noble Eightfold Path. The eight parts are of equal importance. Buddhists aim to practice them all together because they reinforce each other.

The Buddha is in a meditational position.

The Buddha is touching the Earth with his right hand.

9th-century bronze model of a stupa

Theravada Buddhism

Guardian spirits
detail from the
Tipitaka wall
hanging

THERAVADA BUDDHISM IS practiced mainly
in Sri Lanka, Thailand, Laos, Cambodia, and
Burma (also known as Myanmar). Theravada
Buddhists traditionally place the greatest
importance on the Buddha himself and on his
teachings, written in Pali in the ancient scriptures.
The sangha, or community of monks, are also
central to this strand of the faith. In the past,
the practice of meditation was restricted
to monks, who could reach enlightenment.
Ordinary people could only live a life of merit in
the hope of a favorable rebirth. Today, however,
many Theravada Buddhists practice meditation and
hope to move quickly along the path to enlightenment.

*The Tipitaka is being
paraded on the back
of an elephant.*

SPREADING THE WORD
This lion-topped column
is a trademark of the great
Buddhist emperor Ashoka,
who ruled much of India
during the 3rd century
BCE. He built a number
of stupas (pp. 44–45) and
sent his followers across
India to teach others the
dhamma. Ashoka also
constructed many huge
columns inscribed with
Buddhist scriptures and
symbols (pp. 42–43).

TREASURED TIPITAKA
This wall hanging shows a procession in which the Pali scriptures are
carried on the back of an elephant. The scriptures are known as the Tipitaka,
or triple basket, because the manuscripts were originally carried in three
baskets. Each basket held one of the three main parts of the scriptures—
the Vinaya Pitaka, the Sutta Pitaka, and the Abhidhamma Pitaka.

200-year-old palm Pali scriptures in Burmese script bound with cord

PALI ON PALMS
In South and Southeast Asia, Pali scriptures are traditionally written
on pressed palm leaves. Narrow strips of leaves are bound with cords
or ribbons and protected with a wooden cover. Pali is said by some to
be the language used by the Buddha. It is a spoken language with no
script of its own, so can be written in the script of any language.

20th-century
palm scriptures
in a wooden
case bound
with ribbons

WHAT'S INSIDE?

The first of the three parts of the Tipitaka scriptures, the Vinaya Pitaka, includes 227 rules by which Theravada monks must live (pp. 48–51). The second part, the Sutta Pitaka, contains the Buddha's teachings and other writings, such as the Jataka tales. The third and final part, the Abhidhamma Pitaka, is made up of philosophical writings about the Buddhist outlook on life.

FIRST EDITIONS

The scribes who made early copies of the Pali texts used a bronze stylus like this to write on palm leaves. They first prepared the leaves by cutting them to size, boiling them in milk or water, and rubbing them down to produce a smooth, pale finish. They then used the stylus to write out the texts in black ink. Some palm scriptures were highly decorated and coated with gold leaf.

Lacquered palm Tipitaka scriptures in Pali with Burmese script

Ananda's statue stands 23 ft (7 m) tall.

Giant statue of Ananda, Polonnaruwa, Sri Lanka

Modern Pali scriptures containing the Dhammapada

PALI IN PRINT

Modern scriptures like these are often printed on strips of cardboard to mimic earlier palm versions. One of the most popular parts of the Tipitaka today is the Dhammapada. This collection of the Buddha's sayings is part of the Sutta Pitaka. It is full of advice about living well, doing good, and purifying the mind. Many Buddhists learn it by heart.

FAVORITE FOLLOWER

The Buddha's cousin and favorite follower, Ananda, was one of the first arahats, or Buddhist saints. He had not reached enlightenment when the Buddha died, but he did so soon afterward as a result of his deep devotion to the great teacher. All Theravada Buddhists hope to reach enlightenment and become arahats.

Buddhism moves south

Hundreds of golden ornaments adorn the elephant's red velvet costume.

TYPICALLY THAI
In Thailand, the Buddha is often shown making the Earth-witnessing gesture. The tightly curled hair style, pointed headdress, and fine features are also typical of statues of the Buddha from this part of the world.

Dᴜʀɪɴɢ ᴛʜᴇ 3ʀᴅ century ʙᴄᴇ, Buddhism spread southward from India to the island of Sri Lanka. From here, news of the Buddha's life and teachings was carried along the trade routes across the Indian Ocean. It then reached Burma, Thailand, Cambodia, and Laos. Fine temples were built in cities such as Pagan, in Burma, and Angkor, in Cambodia, as the Buddha's teachings were spread all over the region. Theravada Buddhism is popular in these countries to this day. For example, more than 90 percent of the population of Thailand follows this branch of Buddhism.

Buddhists at a religious procession in Kyaukpadoung, Burma

BUDDHIST BURMA
Processions are a notable part of Buddhism in Burma. The tradition began when local rulers became Buddhists as a result of strong links with India and Sri Lanka. They built large temples and took part in lavish ceremonies. Burma is now ruled by the military, but most of the people are still Buddhists.

Burmese-style peace pagoda, Birmingham, UK

BUILDING FOR MERIT
Theravada Buddhism has spread widely. There are now many Burmese-style buildings in the Western world. Burmese temples often have golden roofs, and Shwedagon pagoda in Burma is the world's largest gold-covered building. Buddhists build these monuments in the hope of gaining merit.

TEMPLE OF THE TOOTH
Sri Lanka's most precious relic is the tooth of the Buddha, kept at the Temple of the Tooth in Kandy. The Portuguese invaded Sri Lanka in the early 1500s and claimed to have destroyed the tooth. But locals claimed it was miraculously saved and built the temple to house it.

FANTASTIC FESTIVAL
This elephant and boy are taking part in Esala Perahera. This is a festival held every year in Kandy, Sri Lanka, in honor of the tooth of the Buddha. The festivities last for several nights. The highlight is a procession in which dancers, musicians, and elephants dressed in beautiful, embroidered clothes parade through the streets. One of the elephants carries a case containing the sacred tooth.

The elephant's decorated covering is called a caparison.

Ornate Burmese alms bowl

GENEROUS GIFTS
This ornate alms bowl (p. 51) has a pointed lid that resembles the roof of a Burmese temple. It is typical of the lavish gifts given to Buddhist monks by Buddhist members of the public. Monks live simple lives, but people hope that these rich gifts will earn them merit.

Those taking part in the procession wear white clothing.

"These jars now hold the relics great in virtue, as mountains hold their jeweled ore."

BUDDHACARITA
The relics

23

Mahayana Buddhism

The text is a Chinese translation of the Diamond Sutra.

T HE BRANCH of the faith called Mahayana, or northern, Buddhism developed in the 1st century CE (common era, the term used by non-Christians for AD). It spread across China, Mongolia, and Tibet, before reaching Vietnam, Korea, and Japan. Some Mahayana practices and beliefs differ from those of Theravada Buddhists. Mahayana Buddhists hope to become bodhisattvas (pp. 26–27). They have a more devotional approach both to the Buddha and to the bodhisattvas. They also have some scriptures, known as sutras, not used in Theravada Buddhism.

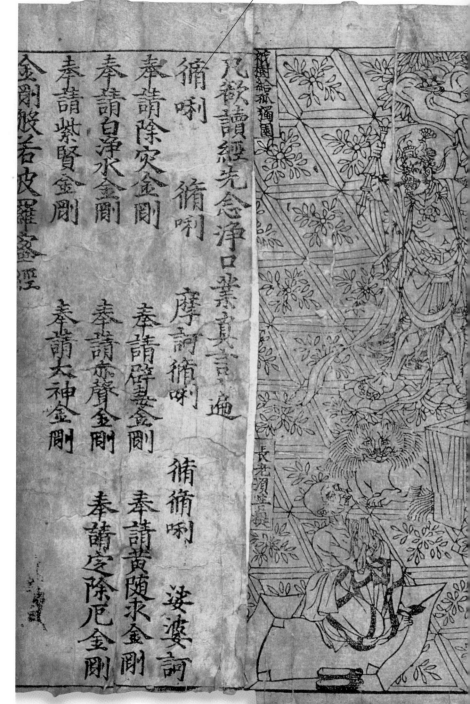

Spirit from the Diamond Sutra

CUTTING WORDS
This Chinese copy of the Diamond Sutra dates from 868. It is the oldest printed book in the world. As with other Mahayana scriptures, the Diamond Sutra was originally written in Sanskrit. Its title suggests that it is able to cut through ignorance like a diamond. The text is a sermon by the Buddha describing a bodhisattva's journey toward wisdom.

7th-century Korean wooden printing block

MIRROR IMAGE
Printing was developed in Korea in order to produce copies of the Mahayana scriptures. The printer had to carve a mirror image of the words of each section into a flat block of wood. This could then be coated with ink and pressed onto a scroll to make a copy of the text.

SHORT, BUT SWEET
The Heart Sutra is a short, very popular scripture. It is recited regularly in numerous Mahayana monasteries, especially the Zen monasteries of Japan (pp. 38–39). The text is known as the "doctrine of emptiness." It says that, in order to become a bodhisattva, a person has first to achieve selflessness through wisdom and compassion.

Painting showing the Heart Sutra being written

The Buddha is making the teaching gesture with his right hand.

The bodhisattvas, with their haloes and crowns, listen to the Buddha's teaching.

Painting of Nagarjuna from the Ki monastery, Spiti, India

LOST AND FOUND

The scholar Nagarjuna was born in India, probably in the 2nd century. According to legend, he discovered and taught sutras that had previously been lost. He founded a school of Buddhism called Madhyamaka, which sought to find a middle way between extremes of thought, belief, and action. It had a huge influence on Mahayana Buddhism.

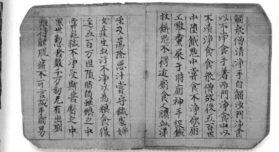

GUARDIAN AND GUIDE

The Lotus Sutra, shown here in Chinese script, describes the Buddha as a being dwelling in a paradise with thousands of faithful followers. He watches over people on the Earth with great compassion. The Lotus Sutra is an example of how skillfully the Buddha's teachings are adapted for people worldwide.

The Buddha wears a symbol of good fortune on his chest.

Many monks listen as the Buddha first speaks the words of the Diamond Sutra.

Wealthy followers of the Buddha have gathered to listen to the sermon.

Fan with text from the Sutra of the Lotus of Good Law

Detail from the Diamond Sutra showing musical spirits called Gandharvas

SIGNIFICANT SUTRAS

The sutras are so important to Mahayana Buddhists that words from them are often written on everyday objects such as fans. Sutra is a Sanskrit word used in Mahayana Buddhism for texts that are written as if spoken by the Buddha himself. These texts include the Pali suttas as well as works written originally in Sanskrit but surviving only in translations.

Other buddhas and bodhisattvas

SIDDHATTA GOTAMA is said to be just one of many buddhas. He was preceded by other people who had, like him, achieved supreme enlightenment and escaped the cycle of life, death, and rebirth. Buddhists believe that there are also people who reach the point of enlightenment but who remain in the realm of ordinary existence. They die and are reborn in order to help others reach enlightenment. These people are known as bodhisattvas. Like the buddhas, they are widely revered, especially in the Mahayana tradition.

AVOIDING ANGER
Akshobya, "the imperturbable" (calm and not excitable), avoided emotions such as anger so that he could achieve any task he set himself. He is said to dwell in a paradise in the east where there is no evil or suffering. He is one of the Jinas, or Cosmic Buddhas (p. 30).

Akshobya's right hand touches the Earth, indicating his enlightenment.

Dipankara's right hand is making the gesture of dhamma, or teaching.

Amoghasiddhi's right hand is in the position that represents fearlessness or blessing.

Vairocana's hands form the dhyana mudra, or meditational gesture.

Amoghasiddhi's left hand rests in his lap in a gesture of meditation.

CREATOR OF LIGHT
The first of the earlier buddhas was called Dipankara, which means "creator of light." A Jataka story tells how the Buddha himself, in an earlier life, met Dipankara and was greatly inspired by his wisdom and compassion.

SPIRITUAL SUCCESS
Amoghasiddhi is one of the Cosmic Buddhas and is most commonly depicted along with the others. This buddha's name means "he who does not work in vain" or "he who is always successful."

UNIVERSAL BUDDHA
Another of the Cosmic Buddhas, Vairocana is seen differently in various branches of Buddhism. For some, he embodies the Historical Buddha; for others, he is a supreme being who embodies the entire universe.

Maitreya, whose name means benevolence or friendship, is known as "the Buddha of the future." It is said that, in thousands of years' time, he will leave the Tushita Heaven, the place where future buddhas dwell. He will then come to the Earth to be the next human buddha.

Maitreya stands, ready to step into the world.

FULL OF MERCY

Renowned for his mercy, Avalokiteshvara is also known as "the protector of the world." He is prepared to be reborn in any form to save living beings from suffering. Although he is widely revered as a male bodhisattva, in eastern Asia, Avalokiteshvara is seen as a female figure. She is known in China as "the goddess of mercy," Kuan Yin (p. 35).

Tara wears the jewels and crown typical of a bodhisattva.

Manjushri holds a sword to cut through ignorance.

MOTHER OF BUDDHAS

Tara, meaning star, is also known as "she who saves." She is greatly revered in Tibet and is referred to as "the mother of all buddhas." Tibetans see her as the ancestor of their people. Tara can take many forms. The best known are the peaceful White Tara and the fierce Green Tara.

THE GENTLE HOLY ONE

The bodhisattva Manjushri, "the gentle holy one," is renowned for his wisdom. In Tibet, great teachers are sometimes said to be incarnations of Manjushri. He is often seen as "the master of all bodhisattvas" and is said to live in a paradise on top of a five-peaked mountain.

Tibetan Buddhism

A DISTINCTIVE type of Mahayana Buddhism developed in Tibet. As in other strands of the Mahayana, Tibetan Buddhists revere the bodhisattvas, in particular Avalokiteshvara and "the mother of all buddhas," Tara. But, like Theravada Buddhists, they place great importance on the role of monks as scholars and teachers. Tibetan Buddhism also has some unique elements, such as the mystical collection of writings and practices known as Tantric Buddhism. When communist China invaded Tibet in 1950, many Buddhist leaders had to leave the country. But this has made the faith stronger, because Tibetan Buddhism has spread all over the world.

FAMILY VALUES
These wooden figures from Tibet show a Buddhist monk and two members of his family. While the monk meditates, the members of his family turn prayer wheels. These figures show the importance of monks and lay people in Tibetan Buddhism—both can achieve buddhahood.

ANCIENT PRACTICES
This 17th-century French illustration shows an ascetic practicing yoga. In the Tibetan strand of Buddhism, meditation is particularly important. The Tibetan word for meditation is "gom." It means to familiarize your mind with something of spiritual significance. Tibetan teachers pass on spiritual knowledge and the teachings of the Buddha through the practice of meditation.

PURE MINDFULNESS
This Tibetan lama (pp. 30–31) is chanting a mantra. A mantra is a word or series of words repeated over and over to help focus the mind during meditation. As the lama concentrates on the rise and fall of his voice and the meaning of the words he is chanting, all other thoughts fall away. He reaches a state of calm and "pure mindfulness."

The lama counts the beads as he chants.

A Tibetan lama's robes are similar in style to those of other monks and nuns (pp. 48–49).

RED HAT, YELLOW HAT

These monks belong to a school of
Tibetan monks called the Gelugpas,
or "Yellow Hats." Monasticism is very
important in Tibetan Buddhism, and
there are four main schools of monks.
The other three schools are the
Nyingmapa, Kargyupa, and Sakya.
These monks all wear red hats.

BUDDHIST BEADS

Many Tibetan Buddhists carry prayer beads to
help them count the number of times they repeat a
mantra or the Triple Refuge (pp. 54–55). Most strings
are made up of 108 beads, which is the number of
desires that must be overcome before reaching
enlightenment. Some prayer beads are made
from the bones of dead holy men or lamas.

Prayer beads made
of ivory, jade,
and sandalwood

*Milarepa holds a hand to
his ear, listening to the
songs he wrote down.*

18th-century
Tibetan bronze
statue of Milarepa

*Milarepa wore
thin, cotton robes
because the type
of meditation
he practiced
generated heat.*

*Protective
cover*

*The weighted
chain helps the
wheel to turn.*

*The scroll
contains a
printed
mantra.*

Complete prayer wheel
(above left) and prayer
wheel opened out to
show how it works

*The metal spindle
holds the scroll.*

SINGING SAINT

Milarepa was a sinner in early life, but he began to regret
his actions and became a Buddhist. Milarepa joined up with
a Buddhist wise man called Marpa. The pair founded the
Kargyupa school of Buddhism, and Milarepa became Tibet's
greatest saint. He wrote down thousands of Buddhist songs
and became a teacher of other holy men.

*The handle
is usually
grasped in the
right hand to
spin the wheel.*

> *"If you have deserved it ...
> a white light will guide you
> into one of the heavens ...
> you will have some happiness
> among the gods."*

TIBETAN BOOK OF THE DEAD
The dawning of the lights of the six places of rebirth

AROUND AND AROUND

Tibetan prayer wheels
contain a roll of paper on
which the sacred mantra
"Om mani padme hum"
("Hail to the jewel in the
lotus") is written many
times. When the wheel
turns, the mantra spins,
in effect being repeated
continuously. This spreads
blessings and well-being and
calls up Avalokiteshvara.

Continued on next page

Tibetan lamas

The most senior monks (pp. 48–51) in Tibetan Buddhism are known as lamas. They are usually people who have achieved mastery of Tibetan-style meditation and the related rituals. Most exalted of all lamas are those known as tulkus. These lamas are believed to be reincarnations of saints or bodhisattvas. They are reborn to teach and to help people to follow the Noble Eightfold Path. Some of the most inspiring of all Buddhist teachers have been lamas and tulkus.

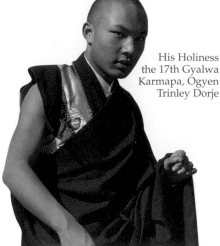

His Holiness the 17th Gyalwa Karmapa, Ogyen Trinley Dorje

ADORED ASHES
These medallions are made from the ashes of lamas who have been cremated after death. The ashes are mixed with clay, formed into discs, and then stamped with an image of the lama. Lamas are widely revered because they devote their lives to spiritual matters.

THE CHOSEN ONES
Toward the end of his life on the Earth, a lama or tulku usually gives clues to help his followers find the site of his next rebirth. After his death, monks follow these hints until they find a child who fits the description. The chosen child, like this young lama, is taken to a monastery to begin a life of study and spirituality.

> *"I now transmit to you the profound teachings which I have myself received from my Teacher and, through him, from the long line of initiated gurus."*
>
> **TIBETAN BOOK OF THE DEAD**
> Preamble

Clay medallions preserving the ashes of venerated Tibetan lamas

Vairocana transforms delusion into wisdom.

Ratnasmbhava transforms pride and greed into wisdom.

Vajrasattva transforms hate into wisdom.

Amitabha transforms lust into wisdom.

Lama's ornate ritual headdress

THE BUDDHAS OF WISDOM
Ritual headdresses worn by lamas are usually decorated with depictions of the Cosmic Buddhas of Mahayana Buddhism. They are also known as "the buddhas of wisdom." These figures are very important because they are said to transform negative emotions into wisdom. This is a quality which, along with compassion, is one of the two most important aspects of enlightenment.

Potala Palace,
Lhasa, Tibet

LAMA IN EXILE
Tenzin Gyatso was declared to be the 14th Dalai Lama in 1937 by the monks of Lhasa. After the Chinese takeover, he was forced to leave Tibet. Since then he has lived in exile, teaching, writing, and campaigning for freedom without violence. He is widely revered, especially in his homeland of Tibet.

POTALA PALACE
This huge palace was built for the Dalai Lama at Lhasa in southern Tibet. The Dalai Lama is the head of the school of Tibetan monks called the Gelugpas. During the 1600s, the Gelugpas became the political, as well as the spiritual, leaders of Tibet. In 1950, Communist China invaded Tibet and brought this unique period of rule to an end.

Ngawang Losang
Gyatso from Samye
monastery, Tibet

MUSIC FOR MEDITATION
This lama is holding a bell and a kind of small drum called a damaru. Tibetan Buddhists use these instruments during rituals. The sounds they produce call on "the bodhisattvas of wisdom," provide musical offerings, and are a focus for meditation.

Tibetan lama
meditating with
a bell and drum

The bell's handle is shaped like a vajra (p. 43).

THE GREAT FIFTH
Ngawang Losang Gyatso (1617–82), the fifth Dalai Lama, was the first lama to rule Tibet. He built the Potala Palace and formed an alliance with the Manchus, the dynasty who ruled neighboring China. He was a powerful but compassionate ruler and is known to Tibetans as the Great Fifth.

The drum is carved from wood and has a brocade tassel.

The bell's beautiful sound is said to awaken the listener from ignorance.

Amoghasiddhi transforms envy into wisdom.

Continued on next page

Tantric Buddhism

This form of Buddhism is based on Tibetan texts called the tantras. It teaches that all thoughts and emotions, even negative ones, are part of the essential buddha-nature—the potential of all beings to reach enlightenment. Under the guidance of a guru, or spiritual teacher, Tantric Buddhists learn to identify with one of the Cosmic Buddhas, hoping to come to a deep understanding of buddha-nature. By using meditation and special rituals Tantric Buddhists aim to reach nibbana much more quickly than other Mahayana Buddhists, who follow the less direct path of the bodhisattvas.

PERFECT WORLD
Tantric Buddhists use complex representations of the Buddhist Cosmos, called mandalas, to help them meditate and reach harmony with buddha-nature. The Buddha Kalachakra sits in the center of this 16th-century mandala with his partner, Vishvamata. They are surrounded by a series of enclosures containing gods and goddesses, making up a perfect world. Tantric Buddhists look at a mandala until they become absorbed in its ideal world and move toward harmony with Kalachakra.

RESISTING EVIL
Hevajra is a form of the Cosmic Buddha Akshobya. He is often shown embracing his partner, Nairatmya, and trampling figures underfoot. Hevajra has five heads, and his sixteen hands hold cups containing gods, ritual objects, and animals. He is an angry deity who uses his terrifying form to fight evil.

Hevajra's left hands hold cups containing gods of the elements, such as water and air.

The central area contains Kalachakra and Vishvamata.

Hevajra's right hands hold cups containing animals.

18th-century bronze statue of Hevajra and Nairatmya

The second area contains 64 goddesses of speech, "the mothers of all mantras."

The third area contains 360 deities in 12 lotus flowers.

"Masters of Tantra" appear along the outer edges of the mandala.

32

He holds a magical staff in his right hand.

Tibetan gilt bronze statue of Padmasambhava

He holds a symbolic weapon in his left hand.

FLOWER CHILD
According to legend, the Indian monk Padmasambhava was born from a lotus blossom and was a form of the Buddha Amitabha. He helped to convert the Tibetans to Buddhism and taught them Tantric rituals. It is said that he used supernatural powers to repel demons who were preventing the spread of Buddhism in Tibet.

CLEARING THE WAY
Tantric Buddhists like these in Nara, Japan, put items such as grains into a fire at their temple. The objects placed in the fire stand for ignorance and for the emotions and thoughts that stand in the way of their enlightenment. The fire destroys the symbolic objects, helping clear the way to nibbana.

TANTRIC TEACHER
Tantric masters guide their followers in meditation, choosing the right methods and practices for each individual. They teach skills such as breath control, the memorizing of mantras, the use of ritual hand gestures called mudras, and the use of mandalas for meditation. All this brings their pupils closer to buddha-nature.

Chinese and Korean Buddhism

BUDDHISM CAME TO China from Central Asia and spread gradually eastward across the country until it reached Korea. At first, there were tensions between Buddhism and established Chinese philosophies such as Confucianism, but the different belief systems learned to live together. They were even combined into a popular religion that saw the bodhisattvas as gods and goddesses who could help people in their everyday lives. China also produced its own schools of Buddhism, some based on intense study, and others based on a simpler path.

Hsüan Tsang mural, Mogao cave temple, Dunhuang, China

Lao Tsu, founder of Taoism, taught people to live a simple, self-sufficient life.

Confucius, founder of Confucianism, taught people to respect others.

The infant Buddha

THREE FAITHS
This 18th-century Chinese painting is an artist's impression of what might have happened if the Buddha had gone to China. Two of the most famous Chinese thinkers, Lao Tsu and Confucius, are shown caring for the infant Buddha. The philosophers had different belief systems, but they respected others, and the three faiths usually got along well in China.

TRAVELING TEACHER
Hsüan Tsang was born in Honan in China. He became a Buddhist monk in the year 620 and made a lengthy pilgrimage across China to India. The journey lasted 16 years and covered more than 40,000 miles (64,000 km). Hsüan Tsang's travels took him through Afghanistan and all around India, where he learned Sanskrit. He translated many scriptures and brought them back to China.

SUTRA STORAGE
This 13th-century lacquered Korean box was made to hold sutras. By the 7th century, Buddhism was flourishing in China, and some emperors were eager to spread the Buddha's teachings around their vast empire. Monks copied the sutras and distributed them across China and into neighboring Korea. These precious manuscripts were often kept in beautiful boxes.

THE COMFORTER
Kuan Yin, the Chinese form of the bodhisattva Avalokiteshvara, inspires love all over China. She is the compassionate "Goddess of Mercy," who listens to the cries of those in distress. Many people keep an image of her in their homes and look upon her as a comforter of those who are sick, lost, or frightened.

LEARNED LOHAN
Chinese Buddhists recognize 18 immortal lohans, or saints. The lohans were followers of the Buddha to whom he entrusted his teachings before his final nibbana. All 18 lohans studied Buddhist law in great depth and eventually achieved enlightenment.

Statue of a lohan from Hebei Province, China

Kuan Yin is usually depicted wearing a crown— a symbol of royalty.

Stucco head of Bodhisattva Kuan Yin dating from the 8th or 9th century

RITUAL CLEANSING
These 12th-century water jars come from Korea, and similar ones are often seen in Korean paintings of the bodhisattva Avalokiteshvara. Monks often sprinkle water during ceremonies to cleanse ritually the statues and people present in the temple. Water containers like this are kept near the altar, or shrine. They are used with a sprinkler made from a willow branch.

Japanese Buddhism

From about the 7th century, travelers began to bring Buddhist ideas to Japan from China and Korea. By this time, there were many different schools of Buddhism in China, all of which were part of the Mahayana strand of the faith. Most Japanese schools of Buddhism, such as Tendai, Shingon, and Jodo Buddhism, are based on forms that began in China. However, one new school, Nichiren Shu, was founded in Japan by a monk who began as a follower of the Tendai school.

TAKING IT EASY
Many different sects of Mahayana Buddhism are popular in Japan, so temples and statues of the Buddha are common and varied. This statue shows the Buddha in the royal ease posture. It is also known as the relaxation posture. It suggests harmony and indicates the Buddha's state of enlightenment.

PURE LAND PARADISE
Amida Buddha is extremely important in the Jodo, or Pure Land, school. Jodo Buddhists believe that Amida, "the Buddha of infinite light," dwells in a Pure Land, or paradise, in the west. Amida has displayed supreme goodness over a vast number of years, and it is said that all who turn to him will be reborn in the Pure Land.

Wooden head of Amida Buddha

PURIFYING FIRE

Rituals practiced by members of the Tendai school include fire ceremonies. Tendai monks pray for 1,000 days—taking only a little sleep and food each day—and tend fires as acts of purification. Some walk across hot ashes to demonstrate that their spiritual purification protects them from injury.

Firewalking ceremony in Hiroshima, Japan

PROTECTIVE POWERS

In Japan, the bodhisattva Avalokiteshvara is called Kannon and is revered by the Tendai, Shingon, Jodo, and other Japanese schools of Buddhism. Kannon can take male or female form. The bodhisattva is often portrayed standing in water, on a fish, or with other sea creatures. This serves as a reminder that Kannon is said to protect sailors and fishermen.

Gilded statue of Kannon

Kannon holds a golden lotus flower in her left hand.

SHARED SHRINE

There is a beautiful Tendai shrine in Nikko in central Japan, decorated with painted animals and gods. It has been a place of pilgrimage for hundreds of years. The shrine at Nikko is sacred to Buddhists and to followers of Japan's native religion, Shinto. It is popular because many Japanese people follow both faiths.

Peacock detail from the shrine in Nikko

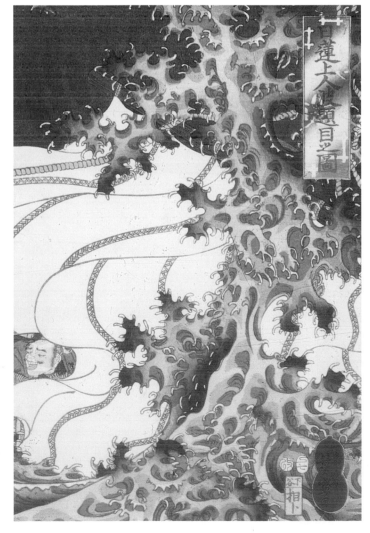

TAKING REFUGE

The Japanese monk Nichiren, seen in this trio of pictures using his faith to calm a storm at sea, was devoted to the Lotus Sutra. He developed a school of Buddhism based on study of the sutra, acceptance of its teachings, and the reciting of the phrase, "I take refuge in the wondrous Sutra of the Lotus."

Zen Buddhism

A FORM OF Buddhism called Ch'an began in China in the 6th century. The school was brought to Japan by a traveling monk called Eisai. The Chinese term Ch'an (which means meditation) became Zen in Japanese. The main feature of Zen is the use of meditation in order to discover the essential buddha-nature that is present in everything and everyone. Zen also has a distinctive style of teaching, often using riddles and stories to help people understand buddha-nature more clearly.

MARATHON MEDITATION
The Indian monk Bodhidharma (right) is said to be the founder of Ch'an Buddhism. He traveled to China to spread the Buddha's teachings and show people how to meditate. According to legend, Bodhidharma meditated in the lotus position for nine years and lost the use of his legs.

SURROUNDED BY BEAUTY
Zen monks, like the one in this Japanese painting on silk, are aware of the beauty and buddha-nature in everything around them. They spend long periods of time meditating in order to encourage natural clarity of mind and move closer to this ever-present buddha-nature.

ABSTRACT ATMOSPHERE

Zen Buddhist temples, and sometimes the homes of Zen Buddhists, have gardens in which arrangements of stones and sand raked into abstract patterns produce a simple, calming effect. The atmosphere created by these Zen gardens is perfect for meditation. In the words of Bodhidharma, it allows Zen Buddhists to "see into their own nature" and perhaps achieve buddhahood.

"Those who perform meditation for even one session destroy innumerable accumulated sins; how should there be wrong paths for them?"

HAKUNI'S SONG OF MEDITATION
Zen meditation

Daitoku-ji temple garden, Kyoto City, Japan

THE ART OF WRITING

For the Chinese, calligraphy, or beautiful writing, is an art form that people practice for many years. Zen scholars in both China and Japan take calligraphy extremely seriously. They concentrate on the beauty of each character as they write it, in the hope that it will be true to the nature of the object or action it portrays.

This character reads "kokoro," which means "heart."

Fukusai-ji Zen temple in Nagasaki, Japan

INTERIOR DESIGN

The interior of this temple in Kyoto, Japan, is in typical Zen style. It is simple and spacious, and decorated with paintings showing natural scenes. There are cushions for the monks to sit on when listening to teachings, and musical instruments such as large gongs for use during ceremonies.

TURTLE-TOPPED

One popular form of Kannon shows the bodhisattva standing on the back of a turtle. At this Zen temple, built in 1979, the whole roof has been built in the form of the turtle's back, with its head outstretched above the door. The statue of Kannon towers above. This is a modern version of traditional Zen buildings, whose large, curving roofs are often the dominant feature.

Demons and gods

BUDDHISM BEGAN IN India among people who believed in many different demons and gods. The Buddha taught that these were beings caught up in the cycle of birth, death, and rebirth, just like humans. These supernatural beings range from gods living in Heaven to demons in the realm of Hell at the very bottom of the Wheel of Life. Some Buddhists believe that all these beings have the power to influence the world. These Buddhists worship the gods in the hope that they will help them in their everyday lives.

SAND GODS
These Tibetan monks are making a mandala from sand of different colors. Each sand mandala is made for a specific ritual and is destroyed afterward. Like other mandalas, sand mandalas are complex images of the Buddhist universe. They feature hundreds of gods and goddesses, each intricately depicted in colored sand.

The protective figure resembles Yama, who holds the Wheel of Life.

INNER DEMONS
In the Buddhist tradition, demons, known as asuras, are fearsome, weapon-wielding creatures who fight the gods. Buddhists in some places see these demons as forces to be feared, and they carry objects like this amulet to protect themselves. Other Buddhists regard the demons as portrayals of the negative feelings we all have, and which we must try to avoid.

Jeweled
Tibetan amulet

A bodhisattva holds the light of hope.

HOPE IN HELL
This section from a Wheel of Life shows Hell—the lowest of the six realms of rebirth. It is a place of torment where beings are tortured in both icy cold and scorching heat. Among the fear and anger in this realm of demons stands a bodhisattva. He preaches a message of hope, which is symbolized by the light of the fire he brings with him.

Realm of desire and possession

LIFE ON THE EARTH
The 12 scenes around the edge of a Wheel of Life depict aspects of life on the Earth. They show figures who stand for different qualities. For example, a blind man represents ignorance, and a man picking fruit represents desire and possession. Many Buddhists look to the gods for help in handling the challenges of life on the Earth.

18th-century engraving of Yama

LORD OF DEATH
Some images of the ancient Indian god Yama show him riding a bull. In others, he has a bull's head. Yama was absorbed into Buddhist culture as "Lord of Death," "King of Hell," and "protector of the Buddhist law." According to some traditions, he judges the dead and takes them to the correct realm to be reborn.

HAPPY IN HEAVEN
This section from a Wheel of Life shows the realm of the gods, or Heaven, where everyone is happy. Trees and flowers flourish, and there are fine palaces and stupas (pp. 44–45). A bodhisattva holding a lute stands at the center. He reminds the gods that when their good kamma runs out they will have to be reborn in a lower realm.

NATURE SPIRITS
This 100-year-old Burmese folding book shows the variety of different forms taken by the demonic beings known as nats. These supernatural beings are nature spirits with a long history in Burma. Like the gods and goddesses of India, nats have been absorbed into local Buddhist belief.

Healing mantras in Burmese script surround the nats.

Indra travels on the back of a white elephant— a form of transportation fit for a king.

11th-century Indian depiction of Indra, "King of the Gods"

KING OF THE GODS
In Hinduism, Indra is "King of the Gods." He holds a similar position among the gods and goddesses of the Buddhist realm of Heaven. Indra is also known as Shakra, "the mighty one," and in some of the sutras he is referred to as Vajrapani. He is a faithful guardian of the Buddha.

Buddhist symbols

In the early days of the Buddhist faith, symbols were often used in place of more complex images. An empty throne, for example, could be used to stand for the Buddha's presence, and a simplified Bodhi Tree could represent the moment of his enlightenment. Symbols have continued to appear in art, on objects, and in buildings. Some symbols are drawn from the natural world. Others may be ritual objects, items associated with the Buddha's life, or symbols that have been adapted from other faiths and traditions.

VOICE OF THE BUDDHA
In India, the conch shell is traditionally blown like a horn to call people to meetings or gatherings. Its low sound carries for long distances. It symbolizes the voice of the Buddha and the way in which his teachings are spread throughout the world.

Chinese enameled vase in the shape of two fish

FERTILE FISH
Fish have thousands of offspring, so in Buddhism these creatures are symbols of fertility. They are usually golden and are often portrayed in pairs, placed head to head. The fish, umbrella, treasure vase, lotus, conch shell, knot, banner, and wheel are the Eight Auspicious (lucky) Symbols of Buddhism.

Ceremonial conch with silk tassel

The knot symbolizes the infinite wisdom of the Buddha.

MAJESTIC ELEPHANT
The elephant is just one of the animals that often appears in Buddhist art. It is a quiet, strong creature that sums up the calm majesty aspired to by Buddhists. A rare white elephant even appears in the story of the Buddha's conception. Other animals appear at the center of the Wheel of Life and as guardians of temples.

PRECIOUS PRINTS
Before his death, the Buddha stood on a rock in Kushinagara in Nepal facing toward the south. When he moved, he is said to have left his footprints in the stone. Ever since, images of these prints have been used as symbols of his presence on the Earth. They appear at many temple sites, where they are treated with special reverence. Pictures and carvings of the footprints are often covered with other Buddhist symbols.

Long, straight toes of even length are said to be one of the 32 marks of a great man.

The swastika is an ancient Indian symbol of good fortune.

Stone footprints from the Amaravati stupa in southern India

The footprints are framed by a border of intertwined lotus flowers.

The Wheel of Authority, which can have up to 1,000 spokes, represents the Buddha as "King of the Dhamma."

This three-pointed symbol represents the Triple Jewel.

Lion guardian at a temple entrance, Birmingham, UK

REACH FOR THE SKY

The lotus is a symbol of spiritual growth. It grows in muddy water, but its stems and flowers reach upward to the Sun, as if toward nibbana. The Buddha is often depicted on a throne made of lotus petals, and people bring lotus flowers as offerings to Buddhist shrines (pp. 52–53).

GUARDIAN LION

As Buddhism spread around the world, it adopted traditional symbols from the places where it took root. The use of lion statues to guard temples was originally a Chinese tradition. Many Buddhist temples now have lion guardians at their entrances.

PROTECTION AND POWER

In the Buddha's time, members of royalty were protected from the rain and sun by umbrellas held by servants. The umbrella became a symbol of protection and the Buddha's spiritual power. Stupas are often topped with umbrella-shaped carvings called finials (pp. 44-45).

SPIRITUAL WEAPON

Translated as either "diamond" or "thunderbolt," the vajra is a symbolic weapon. It is said to be able to cut through any substance. It is used, especially in Tibet, as a symbol of the spiritual power that can cut through ignorance. Some Buddhists hold the vajra in one hand and a bell in the other while chanting.

Vajra-shaped handle

Tibetan bell

Tibetan vajra

Modern Buddhist parade umbrella

The umbrella is made of golden paper decorated with colored thread.

Stupas and pagodas

AFTER THE BUDDHA died, his body was cremated. His ashes were divided and buried in a number of different places in India. A large, dome-shaped mound called a stupa was built over the relics, or remains, at each burial place. Later, many other stupas were built all over the Buddhist world. Some were constructed over the remains of Buddhist saints, and others were built over copies of the scriptures. Many existing stupas were clad with decorative carved stone and given elaborate gateways. They soon became popular places of pilgrimage (p. 54). In China, Japan, and parts of Southeast Asia, tall structures called pagodas developed from the stupa form.

LITTLE AND LARGE
Model stupas like this are used for personal devotion at home. When visiting a full-size stupa, Buddhists walk around it as an act of respect to the relic kept there.

IN RUINS
This structure was built in the 5th century in Sarnath near Benares. It marks the site where the Buddha gave his first sermon. The stupa is now in ruins. The large, dome-shaped covering on the top has not survived, but the carved lower walls are still intact. The first stupa at this important site was built by the great Indian emperor Ashoka in the 3rd century BCE.

A row of pillars, called ayaka, top the gateway through which pilgrims would enter the stupa.

The gateway is guarded by lions.

A rich young man has come to the stupa to make an offering.

The stone cladding and gateway were added after Ashoka's time.

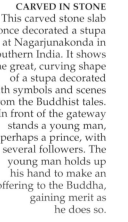

MAKING AMENDS
This stupa, on the site of an early monastery in Sanchi in India, was built by the emperor Ashoka. He became a Buddhist after leading his army into a battle in which thousands were killed. Ashoka regretted the violence and devoted himself to spreading Buddhism and erecting thousands of stupas and shrines.

CARVED IN STONE
This carved stone slab once decorated a stupa at Nagarjunakonda in southern India. It shows the great, curving shape of a stupa decorated with symbols and scenes from the Buddhist tales. In front of the gateway stands a young man, perhaps a prince, with several followers. The young man holds up his hand to make an offering to the Buddha, gaining merit as he does so.

19th-century illustration of Borobudur

SUPER STUPA

Borobudur is an enormous stupa in Java. The lower levels are richly decorated with relief carvings showing scenes from the Buddha's life. The upper levels are plainer, and contain a series of smaller stupas. Each of the small stupas on the upper levels contains a statue of the Buddha.

The umbrella-shaped finial is a symbol of kingship that stands for the Buddha's spiritual rule.

Spirits offer garlands of flowers to the Buddha.

A carving of the Buddha marks the center of the stupa.

"There, with the appropriate ceremonies, they erected in their capital cities stupas for the relics of the Seer."

BUDDHACARITA
The relics

Engraving of a Chinese pagoda

TALL AND BEAUTIFUL

In China, Japan, and Korea, Buddhist relics are housed in pagodas. Chinese and Korean pagodas are usually built of stone or brick. Those in Japan are wooden. A long pole inside connects the relics buried at the base to the top of the structure. Pagodas are stunning buildings. They are often very tall and have ornate roofs with delicate, upturned corners.

Temples and complexes

Above one of the entrances to the Baiju temple in Gyantse in Tibet, there is a mural of the Buddha's eyes, with the urna between them. The half-open eyes seem to watch over those who enter the temple. At the same time, they bring to mind a state of deep meditation.

ALL BUDDHIST TEMPLES contain statues of the Buddha. They are places in which Buddhists can gather and make offerings, and they also provide a focus for devotion and pilgrimage. Buddhist temples vary greatly in shape and size. Some are quite small, comprising just an entrance area and a simple inner shrine. Others are huge complexes, which may consist of many small stupas containing relics. Some temples are plain and unadorned. Others, such as the Mahabodhi temple at Bodh Gaya and the temples on the Silk Road in Central Asia, are decorated with stunning carvings and paintings.

Mahabodhi temple, Bodh Gaya, India

The main tower is covered with detailed carvings.

TEMPLE BY THE TREE
The Mahabodhi temple at Bodh Gaya is one of the most important destinations of Buddhist pilgrimage. It marks the site where the Buddha became enlightened. Building work started in the 6th century next to a tree that is believed to be a descendant of the one under which the Buddha meditated. The large temple complex fell into disrepair between the 13th and 19th centuries, but was eventually restored and extended by monks and pilgrims.

The small stupas match the shape of the main tower.

Some of the miniature stupas contain the ashes of pilgrims who died in Bodh Gaya.

FACE TOWERS
The Bayon in Angkor in Cambodia is a beautiful temple built by the Khmer king Jayavarman VII (1181–1219). The enormous faces carved in the walls of the Bayon are said to represent the bodhisattva Avalokiteshvara, but they may be based on the features of Jayavarman himself.

CARVED IN CLIFFS
In Ellora, in the northwest of India's central Deccan region, more than 30 temples have been carved into the local cliffs. People cut their way through tons of solid rock to hollow out large halls and shrines. Pillars, statues, and vaulted ceilings have also been carved from the rock inside the cave temples.

Vajravira holds a staff above his head.

Vajravira's body is protected by golden armor.

Vajravira at the Taiyuin-byo shrine in northern Honshu

CROSSING THE STREAM
The walls and roof of this small temple in Ayuthaya in Thailand are reflected in the nearby water. As well as enhancing the beauty of the temple's surroundings, the water is an important symbol. Buddhists sometimes use the phrase "crossing the stream" to describe the process of passing through the world of suffering on the way to enlightenment.

GREEN GUARDIAN
This figure, Vajravira, is one of the Four Guardian Kings. Found guarding entrances or shrines, especially in Japanese temples, the Guardian Kings are said to protect the four points of the compass. They are usually shown as warriors, wearing armor, brandishing weapons, and trampling on demons. Vajravira protects the west and can be identified by his green skin.

This detail is called a cho fa, or "tassel of air."

The bargeboards are ornately carved.

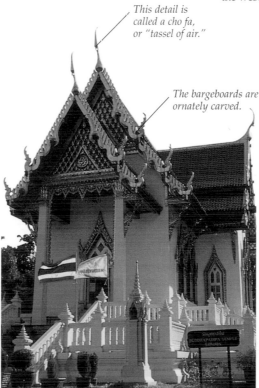

"When you have performed the acts of worship, help will come from the guardian angels."

BYA CHOS
The Buddha's law among the birds

WESTERN TEMPLE EASTERN STYLE
This British Buddhist temple, like many in the West, is built in a style influenced by the architecture of Southeast Asia. The pitched roofs, pointed windows, and carved details give the building an Eastern appearance. The "tassels of air" are said to be based on simplified statues of the bird Garuda, a Hindu god who protected people from evil.

Buddhist monks and nuns

SOME BUDDHISTS JOIN the community of monks and nuns called the sangha. They devote their lives to understanding the Buddha's teachings and explaining them to others. In order to join the sangha, Buddhists take part in a ceremony called ordination. They promise to observe a set of rules that affect everything they do. Buddhist monks and nuns live simple lives. They wear plain robes, shave their heads, study, and meditate.

Needle and thread

Razor

Water strainer

Alms bowl

Lid from alms bowl, used as a plate

WOMEN'S RIGHTS
In most branches of Buddhism, women like this Tibetan nun may be ordained and become members of the sangha. Some of these nuns have become important spiritual leaders. Women can become nuns in all traditions of Buddhism, but in Theravada Buddhism, nuns have a lower status than monks.

FEW THINGS
Buddhist monks are allowed to have very few possessions. The basics are robes, a place to live, an alms bowl, and medicine. They may also own a razor, a needle and thread for mending their robes, a belt, and a strainer to ensure that insects are not swallowed along with drinking water.

Lower robe, worn around the hips

Upper robe, worn over the shoulder

Outer robe, worn for travel and sleeping

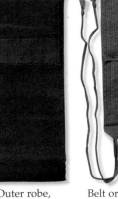
Belt or girdle

COMMON COLOR
Monks' robes are traditionally dyed a saffron, or orangey-yellow, color, as seen in this Thai mural. This is said to date back to the time when the Buddha founded the sangha. He and his followers made their robes by sewing together scraps of cloth and dyeing them a common color.

ROBE RULES
A Buddhist monk is allowed three robes made of plain, dyed material. The color of the robes varies according to the branch of Buddhism. In the Theravada tradition, the robes are yellow or orange. Tibetan monks wear maroon robes, and Zen members of the sangha wear black.

Both monks and novices shave their heads.

The upper robe is worn covering only the left shoulder within the monastery.

Thai novice monk in his simple hut

LET US BE HAPPY
In the early days of Buddhism, many monks lived in caves or other simple shelters. They spent much of their lives traveling from place to place. Monks and nuns today usually live in permanent monasteries, but they still live simple lives. A monk's life should be one of fulfillment. As one scripture says, "Let us be happy, then, we who possess nothing."

The upper robe is tied firmly around the novice's body.

These robes are made from cotton, but the scriptures also allow other plant-based fabrics to be used.

Traditionally, the robes are colored using dyes derived from clay, plants such as the saffron flower, and other natural materials.

IN IT FOR LIFE
Boys as young as seven or eight may enter monasteries as novices. They learn about the dhamma and can be ordained as monks in their late teens. Not all monks stay in the monastery for life. In some places, it is traditional for young men to spend anything from a few weeks to several years in a monastery. During this time, they are educated and acquire merit. Other Buddhists dedicate their entire lives to the sangha.

Thai Buddhist monk with two novices

Monks and novices traditionally go barefoot.

Continued on next page

The monastic way of life

Buddhist monks and nuns agree to obey more than 200 rules, covering everything from their relations with other people to the clothes they wear and the food they eat. They give up sexual contact, live in monasteries, and practice meditation. Monks and nuns, however, are not isolated from the world. In addition to teaching, some members of the sangha help to run health clinics, take care of orphaned children, or care for the elderly and the sick.

"The homeless wanderer ... is content with little, easily pleased ... not addicted to society, energetic, independent, solitary, perfect in his conduct ..."

MILINDAPANHA
Laymen and monks

DAILY DUTIES
Every day, monks like these in Thailand meet to chant verses from the sutras to honor the Buddha. They may also recite the monastic rules to remind them of the discipline under which they live. Buddhist monks also meditate regularly. This trains their minds to become calm and encourages right effort, right mindfulness, and right concentration.

TIME TO TEACH
Buddhist monks spend a lot of their time teaching others about the dhamma. The Buddha depended on his followers to pass on his ideas. This teaching can take different forms. It may involve explaining the texts of Buddhist scriptures or showing people how the Buddha's ideas can help them overcome their problems.

Fans were originally carried to help monks keep cool in hot climates.

The monk sits in the half-lotus position when teaching.

ACCEPTING ALMS

Many monks and nuns accept alms, or gifts. Alms are donated by lay people—Buddhists who are not members of the monastic sangha. In the early days of Buddhism, monks had to depend entirely on alms for survival. Rich lay Buddhists then began making gifts of land to groups of monks. Strictly speaking, this is against monastic rules, but it allows monks and nuns to settle down, build monasteries, and grow their own food.

Rice and lotus flower offerings

The outer robe is worn outside the monastery.

The alms bowl is held out ready to receive food.

GIVING AND RECEIVING

In places where monks still rely upon direct gifts from lay people, they hope for practical alms of things like food and medicine. Such gifts also help those who give. By giving, lay people gain merit that will lead them toward better rebirths and perhaps membership of the sangha in a future life.

Monks are not allowed to take gifts directly in their hands.

MORNING STROLL

In places such as Thailand, monks still spend part of each day walking through the streets so that people can place food into their alms bowls. This daily alms round takes place in the morning so that the monks can gather enough food for their main meal, which they have to eat before midday.

Burmese nuns discussing the scriptures

GROUP STUDY

Monks and nuns study regularly, often meeting to discuss the scriptures. Members of the sangha have always preserved and studied Buddhist scriptures. In the early days, they did this by reciting them aloud; later, they wrote out texts by hand. Today, the texts are printed in books and available on the internet.

Monk collecting alms

The Buddhist way of life

BUDDHISTS REGULARLY visit temples to make offerings, but their faith goes further than this. It affects their whole lives. When the Buddha described the Noble Eightfold Path, he meant for its eight parts to influence every activity. Whether Buddhists are at home, at work, or on vacation they try to live according to their beliefs. Above all, Buddhists try to act in a caring way. They think positively, help others, and promote peace. In doing so, they hope to build up merit to improve their next rebirth. Buddhists also hope to make the world a better place for everyone to live in.

Stone carving showing two princes and a monk offering flowers to the Buddha

ONE OF MANY
There are a very large number of Buddhist shrines and temples. One reason for this is that putting up a new one is a way for lay people to gain merit. A rich person might pay for a whole temple. Poorer people can join groups to collect funds for building, or build simple shrines like this.

GIVE IT UP
Making offerings to the Buddha is one of the most familiar rituals for lay Buddhists like the princes shown in this carving. It is a symbolic way of following in the footsteps of the Buddha himself, because in his previous lives he gave up his possessions, and sometimes even his life, to help others.

Burning incense sticks

Chinese bronze incense pot

ODOROUS OFFERINGS
One way to make an offering is to do so by burning the aromatic substance incense. Doing this allows lay people to build up merit, which will help to ensure a favorable rebirth. In a similar way, Tantric Buddhists sometimes make offerings of fire.

MERIT SHARING
These vessels are used for a merit-sharing ceremony in which water is poured slowly from one vessel to the other while chanting takes place. Buddhists traditionally consider people to be responsible for their own merit. But it is possible to share merit, for example, by passing it on to a dead person in the hope that a better rebirth will result.

Water vessels used for merit sharing

Pineapple

Papaya

Banana

FRUITFUL GIFTS
Lay people may make offerings of fruit and other foods directly to the Buddha by placing them on a shrine. They can also offer them to monks in the form of alms. Providing that the fruit is clean and offered sincerely, the variety is not important.

Rice offering from a Tibetan Buddhist shrine

REVERED RICE
Rice is a common and welcome gift for Buddhist monks in Asia. It is a nourishing food and a symbol of blessing. Rice is also one of the offerings most often placed on shrines for the Buddha. Buddhists hope that in return for the rice offerings their community will be blessed with enough food. The rice placed on shrines should be changed every full moon. The old rice is taken outside and fed to birds, fish, or other animals.

This elaborate container for rice offerings is made to look like a stupa.

Laundry day, Holy Island, Scotland

Gardening, Holy Island, Scotland

Preparing food, Holy Island, Scotland

MERIT IN THE MUNDANE
A Buddhist's beliefs affect every aspect of his or her life. Even everyday tasks like doing laundry, gardening, and cooking should be carried out in a way that is mindful of the Buddha's teachings and does not harm others. Many Buddhists do not eat meat because this involves killing living things. Some Buddhists do not even dig in the soil for fear of harming any creatures living in it.

REACHING OUT
This Buddhist monk is working with prisoners in the UK. He tells them about the Buddha's teachings and explains why it is wrong to harm others. Monks also build gardens in prison grounds, creating peaceful spaces for inmates to visit. Some convicted criminals change their way of life as a result of this work.

PEACE PROTEST
These Buddhist monks and nuns are demonstrating against the war in Kosovo in 1999. Buddhists oppose killing and most believe in ahimsa, or nonviolence. They will not fight in wars, and often take part in antiwar protests.

Devotion to the Buddha

THE BUDDHA IS an enlightened being, not a god, so he is not worshipped in the way gods are worshipped in other religions. Buddhists do have great respect for the Buddha. They perform rituals of devotion to confirm their commitment to the Buddha, his dhamma, and the sangha. This is known as the Triple Refuge. Buddhists express their devotion in various ways. They make pilgrimages, meditate, give offerings, and prostrate themselves. In each case, the act of devotion also serves to help the devotees. It encourages them to follow the dhamma and reminds them of the Eightfold Path.

FOOTPRINT FOCUS
Images like this one of the Buddha's footprint provide a focus for devotion. The footprint features many key Buddhist symbols and some of the marks of a great man. It reminds Buddhists of the Buddha's remarkable life and teaching.

The case is ornately carved and decorated with jewels.

SPIRITUAL SITES
These Buddhists have made a pilgrimage to Shwedagon pagoda in Burma, where some relics of the Buddha are kept. Buddhists visit places linked with the life of the Buddha, shrines where relics are kept, and other sites with spiritual links. Pilgrimages are especially important to lay people. They allow them to follow in the Buddha's footsteps and to focus on spiritual matters.

JOY AND CONTEMPLATION
This case was used to preserve a relic of a Buddhist saint. Buddhists have always revered the relics of the Buddha and of notable teachers and saints. Pilgrimages to relics of the Buddha can be times of joyful celebration of his life and teaching, but also times of quiet contemplation and spiritual growth.

Prostration and meditation

Prostration is usually performed before a statue of the Buddha. It is repeated three times as a dedication to the Triple Refuge. It is an expression of reverence and helps Buddhists to develop qualities such as humility. Meditation is a vital part of the Buddhist faith. The calm and focused state it provokes brings the devotee closer to wisdom and even enlightenment.

1 DEDICATED BODY
Standing facing a statue of the Buddha, this lama puts his hands together, with the fingers touching and the palms slightly cupped. He raises his hands to his forehead to demonstrate that his body is dedicated to the Triple Refuge.

2 RIGHT SPEECH
Still in the standing position, the lama lowers his hands to just below his mouth to show that he devotes his speech to the Triple Refuge. In doing this, he also recalls the third part of the Eightfold Path—right speech.

The lama clasps his robe to prevent it from falling.

3 DEVOTED HEART AND MIND
Next, the lama lowers his hands farther so that they are in front of his chest. This position shows that his heart, and therefore also his mind, are devoted to the Triple Refuge. He then prepares to prostrate himself.

The lama kneels on all fours before sliding to the floor.

The lama is now fully prostrated.

4 PROSTRATION POINTS
The lama kneels down and places his palms on the floor. From this point, he performs a full prostration with his whole body lowered to the floor. Many Buddhists perform a five-point prostration instead. On all fours, they lower their foreheads to the floor so that five parts of their body—their lower legs, their forearms, and their forehead—are in contact with the floor.

A comfortable posture is essential for meditation.

Gong

Hammer

FREEING THE MIND
Meditation clears and purifies the mind. It leads Buddhists to right effort, right mindfulness, and right concentration—three parts of the Eightfold Path. Most Buddhists begin meditation by focusing on their breathing. In some branches of Buddhism, devotees concentrate on an image or object to help them to free their minds from everyday thoughts. Others bang a gong after meditating to spread the merit earned by their act of devotion.

Buddhist festivals

Buddhist dancing figure

BUDDHISM HAS adapted to the many different places where it has taken root, so its festivals vary from one country to another. The various schools of the faith also celebrate different festivals. Theravada Buddhists, for example, mark the birth, enlightenment, and death of the Buddha with a single festival. They also have set days throughout the year when lay people join monks in fasting and meditation. Mahayana Buddhists have a variety of festivals, including celebrations at the New Year and separate ones for the key stages in the Buddha's life.

JOYFUL JIG
Dance is important in many Eastern cultures, and this tradition has carried over into Buddhism. For lay people, dancing is part of many of the more joyful Buddhist festivals, such as those celebrating the New Year and the Buddha's birth. Monks and nuns do not dance.

WATER FESTIVAL
Water plays an important part in New Year celebrations in several Buddhist countries. Images of the Buddha are washed and people bathe or are sprinkled with water. This 19th-century painting shows an elaborate New Year's water festival in Burma. The use of water helps people start the New Year in a state of spiritual purity and cleanliness.

People fill pots with water in preparation for the festivities.

Monk washing statues of the Buddha in London, UK

The shrine is scattered with petals.

FREEING THE FISH
This Thai Buddhist is releasing a captive eel into the wild to mark the festival of Vesak, or Buddha Day. Vesak is a Theravada celebration of the birth, enlightenment, and death of the Buddha. It is a time for being especially kind to living things. In Thailand, some people avoid farm work in which living creatures may be harmed and release captive animals to build up merit.

CEREMONIAL CLEANING
In some temples, Vesak is marked by the ceremonial cleaning of statues of the Buddha as a child. People then make offerings of flowers and incense. Lights are lit in temples and trees to symbolize the Buddha's enlightenment. Parades, Jataka readings, and plays reenacting the Buddha's birth also take place in some areas.

A golden statue of the Buddha is central to the festivities.

Devotees prostrate themselves before the Buddha.

CONVERTING THE KING

In Sri Lanka, monks and lay people gather for a special festival called Poson. This is to celebrate the arrival of Buddhism on the island during the time of the Indian emperor Ashoka. The gathered Buddhists make offerings at Mihintale, where Ashoka's son, Mahinda, is said to have converted the king of Sri Lanka to the faith.

FLOWER POWER

The Japanese celebrate the Buddha's birth at the festival of Hana Matsuri. People make whole gardens of paper flowers as a reminder of the lush gardens in Lumbini, where the Buddha was born. In Japan, perfumed tea is poured over statues of the Buddha because it is said that the gods provided scented water for Siddhatta's first bath.

Japanese children preparing paper flowers for Hana Matsuri

MASKED MONKS

Tibetan New Year is celebrated at the festival of Losar. People wear new clothes and eat special foods, such as cakes called kapse. At the end of the festival, Buddhist monks put on fearsome masks. They then perform a ritual to frighten away any evil spirits that have appeared during the previous year.

The cycle of life

ALL RELIGIONS DEVELOP ceremonies to mark the key stages in a person's life. In Buddhism, two kinds of ceremonies have special importance. The first are rituals of initiation, in which a child or teenager is welcomed into adult Buddhist society and becomes a part of the monastic community for a short while. The second are funeral rites that mark a person's passing from life and signal their future rebirth. Buddhism has spread so widely around the world that these ceremonies vary greatly. But they are all occasions during which Buddhists meet to share a special moment and celebrate their faith.

LITTLE PRINCES
These boys are having their initiation ceremony at the Shwedagon pagoda in Rangoon, Burma. After this, they will join the monastery for a short period. Unlike boys in some other Buddhist countries, they are not immediately given monks' robes to wear. They are dressed in rich clothes, like those Siddhatta wore before leaving his father's palace to seek enlightenment.

BIRTH BLESSINGS
Some Buddhist monks, like this one in the UK, invite new parents to have their babies blessed. But Buddhism does not place great importance on rituals to mark the birth of a child. Parents who wish to mark their child's arrival often use local traditional rituals. Monks are not necessarily involved in these ceremonies.

The monk uses his razor to shave the boy's head.

Mural from Wat Bowornivet temple, Bangkok, Thailand

COMING OF AGE
Before they can be accepted as full members of the Buddhist community, young boys are taken to their local monastery. Monks shave their heads and give them an alms bowl and robes. They stay at the monastery, sometimes just for one night, but often for several days. At the end of this period the boys are no longer regarded as children.

Buddhist nun
blessing a
marriage

RELIGIOUS REMINDER
Buddhism stresses the importance of the role
and life of monks and nuns, so weddings are not
looked on as religious events. Buddhist couples
choose to have a civil, or nonreligious, ceremony
sometimes followed by a blessing from a monk
or nun. The blessing reminds the couple that
the sangha will remain important in their lives.

Lotus
flowers

Candle

FAMILY FAVORS
When a person dies, relatives usually make
offerings such as flowers and candles to the
local monks. They gain merit by doing this,
and hope that the merit will be transferred
to the deceased, helping them on the way
to a more favorable rebirth.

FUNERAL TRADITIONS
When Buddhists die, they
are usually placed in caskets
decorated with cloths and
flowers. They are then taken
in a procession to the temple,
where monks chant scriptures
concerning kamma and
rebirth. In the Theravada
tradition, the deceased
person is usually cremated,
as the Buddha was, but
Mahayana Buddhists
bury their dead.

Funeral procession
in Burma

Stupa-shaped
case for relics
from Bihar
in India

*"Sweet-scented barks
and leaves, aloewood,
sandalwood, and
cassia they heaped on
the pyre, sighing with
grief all the time.
Finally they placed the
Sage's body on it."*

BUDDHACARITA
The relics

IN THE NEXT LIFE
This ornate stupa-shaped
case was probably made
to hold the cremated remains
of a notable Buddhist saint or
teacher. The cremation is the
climax of Theravada funeral
services. Family members
usually keep the ashes in
an urn. After the funeral,
the relatives may burn the
favorite possessions of
the deceased so that he
or she can enjoy them
in the next life.

STAYING POSITIVE
Although it is sad when
a friend or relative dies,
funerals are positive
occasions for Buddhists
because they lead to a
rebirth. Ceremonies to
honor the deceased
may involve burning
incense. This reminds
those present of the
Buddha's enlightened
teaching that death is
merely an interval
between two lives.

Buddhist culture

Chinese laughing Buddha statue

BUDDHISM HAS flourished during the 20th and 21st centuries. Many new Buddhist movements have been founded in Asia, and a large number of Asian Buddhists have traveled to the West, bringing their ideas with them. Many Western people have become Buddhists, encouraged in part by movements such as the Friends of the Western Buddhist Order, founded in the UK. As a result, there has been a worldwide spread of Buddhist culture involving everything from meditation to movies and art. This cultural spread has influenced a huge number of people, many of whom are not Buddhists.

ORNAMENTAL BUDDHAS
People worldwide own statues of the Buddha. Even non-Buddhists admire their spirituality and calm. This is a Chinese representation of Maitreya, "the Buddha of the future." It is an adaptation of their god of wealth and prosperity.

MEDITATION FOR RELAXATION
All followers of the Buddha meditate, but today many other people do as well. Non-Buddhists do not hope to reach enlightenment through meditation, but they do value the way in which meditation enables them to rid their minds of troubling or confusing thoughts. After a session of meditation, people find they are happier and more able to face their problems.

Non-Buddhist meditating in a semilotus position

POPULAR POT PLANTS
The ancient Japanese practice of bonsai involves restricting the growth of trees by techniques such as pruning and confining them to small pots. Bonsai was adopted by the Zen tradition because the living materials are used in a contemplative way to create beautiful, natural forms.

Japanese woman creating an ikebana display

ELEGANT OFFERINGS
Buddhist flower offerings do not have to be presented in an elaborate way, but Japanese Buddhists developed a tradition for beautifully arranged offerings. Ikebana grew from this practice. These elegant arrangements are now popular among non-Buddhists worldwide.

> *"Think of not thinking of anything at all. Be without thoughts— this is the secret of meditation."*

CONTROLLING THE MIND
Zen meditation

GOLDEN BOY
This section from a shrine frieze in Bangkok, Thailand, includes an image of British soccer player David Beckham (above right). Normally, only gods, bodhisattvas, and saints would be featured in this kind of frieze. But Beckham is a figure from popular culture with a reputation that has won him a place among the gods.

FAMILY AFFAIR
Actress Uma Thurman comes from a Buddhist family. Her father, a professor of Indo-Tibetan Buddhist studies, was the first Westerner to become a Tibetan Buddhist monk. Uma is not a practicing Buddhist but, like many people, she says that the faith has had a major influence on her life.

GOING PUBLIC
Famous Buddhists like Hollywood actor Richard Gere have helped to introduce Buddhism to a wider public in the West. Gere became a Buddhist following a trip to Nepal in 1978. Since then, he has been a tireless campaigner for religious freedom in Tibet. He is a supporter of the Dalai Lama and other Tibetan Buddhist exiles.

Continued on next page

Buddhism in the Arts

The Buddha and his ideas have inspired artists for hundreds of years. Sculptors and painters have produced countless images of the Buddha, ranging from small pictures for display indoors to large outdoor statues that can be seen from great distances. Artists in many fields, from illustrators to filmmakers, are inspired by Buddhism. They tell stories and paint pictures based on Buddhist teachings, on the lives of Buddhist monks or nuns, and on the role of Buddhism in modern life.

BIG BUDDHA
This enormous statue is the largest seated Buddha in the world. It was carved out of the rock face of Lingyun Hill in Leshan in China in about 800. The statue represents the Buddha Maitreya, who sits with his hands on his knees. It is a popular attraction for both tourists and pilgrims, drawing more than 300,000 visitors a year.

The statue is about 230 ft (70 m) tall and the shoulders measure 90 ft (30 m) across.

PAST GLORY
The world's two largest standing Buddhas were in Bamiyan in Afghanistan. The larger of the two was more than 185 ft (55 m) tall. By 400, there were many monasteries and thousands of monks in Bamiyan. But the monasteries went into decline when the area converted to Islam. In 2001, the huge Buddhas were destroyed by the Taliban, who were then in power.

SIGN OF THE TIMES
Kinkaku-ji pagoda at Kansai in Japan was built in 1955 on the site of a 14th-century Buddhist temple. Building stupas and pagodas is a way of gaining merit, so many have been rebuilt a number of times. Instead of the steeply upturned roof lines of more traditional pagodas, Kinkaku-ji's lines are straighter, like other city structures built in the 1950s.

The figure is so large that 100 people can stand on one of its enormous feet.

PEACE MAKER

This modern painting by Liz Wright is called East Meets West. It is a version of the story of the patron saint of England, Saint George, and the Dragon. In the original story George kills the dragon, who has been devouring innocent people. In this picture the Buddha sits on the dragon's back and raises his arm to stop George. It is as if the Buddha is trying to make peace between the enemies.

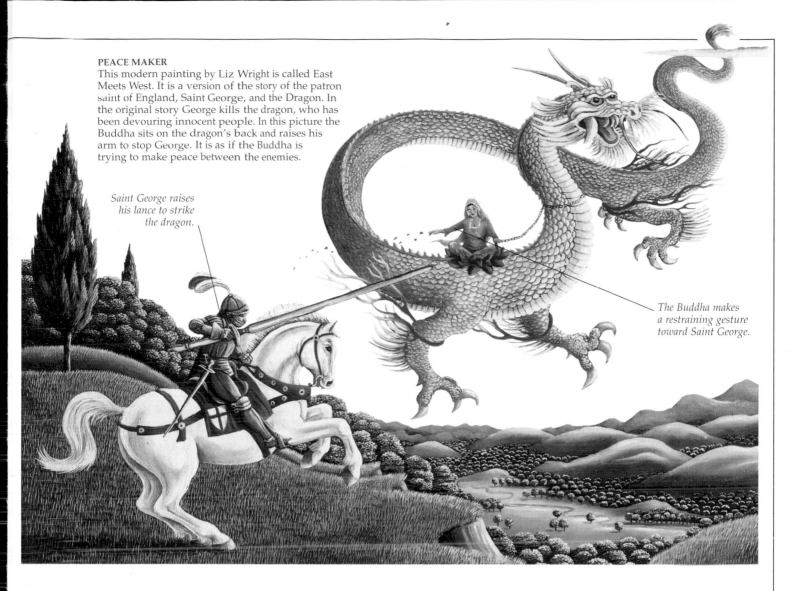

Saint George raises his lance to strike the dragon.

The Buddha makes a restraining gesture toward Saint George.

SHINING LIGHT

In this modern painting from India, the Buddha is shown sitting beneath the Bodhi Tree. The halo of light around his head suggests that he has achieved enlightenment. The forefinger and thumb of his right hand touch to make the dhamma gesture—a sign that he is ready to start teaching.

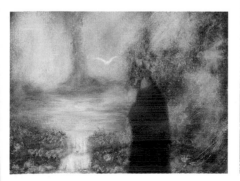

ARTIST'S IMPRESSION

Buddhism has a rich store of images that are inspiring to some modern artists. This stylized oil painting shows a Tibetan monk in his maroon robe. He is surrounded by birds, flowers, and water. This symbolizes the respect and reverence that Buddhists have for the natural world and all living things.

LIFE STORY

Little Buddha is a film by Italian director Bernardo Bertolucci. It tells the story of a group of monks who go in search of the reincarnation of a great Buddhist lama. The person they find is a small boy living in Seattle. The film also tells the life story of the Buddha himself.

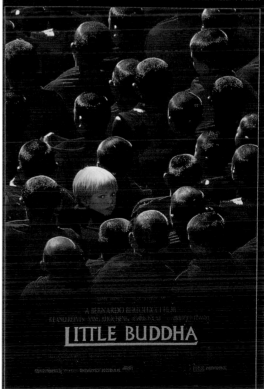

FROM BERNARDO BERTOLUCCI - CREATOR OF "THE LAST EMPEROR" COMES A MAGICAL JOURNEY TO A PLACE WHERE THE PAST AND THE PRESENT MEET.

LITTLE BUDDHA

1 BIRD
2 ROCKS & MINERALS
3 SKELETON
4 ARMS & ARMOR
5 TREE
6 POND & RIVER
7 BUTTERFLY & MOTH
8 SPORTS
9 SHELL
10 EARLY HUMANS
11 MAMMAL
12 MUSIC
13 DINOSAUR
14 PLANT
15 SEASHORE
16 FLAG
17 INSECT
18 MONEY
19 FOSSIL
20 FISH
21 CAR
22 FLYING MACHINE
23 ANCIENT EGYPT
24 ANCIENT ROME
25 CRYSTAL & GEM
26 REPTILE
27 INVENTION
28 WEATHER
29 CAT
30 BIBLE LANDS
31 EXPLORER
32 DOG
33 HORSE
34 FILM
35 COSTUME
36 BOAT
37 ANCIENT GREECE
38 VOLCANO & EARTHQUAKE
39 TRAIN
40 SHARK
41 AMPHIBIAN
42 ELEPHANT
43 KNIGHT
44 MUMMY
45 COWBOY
46 WHALE
47 AZTEC, INCA & MAYA
48 BOOK
49 CASTLE
50 VIKING
51 DESERT
52 PREHISTORIC LIFE
53 PYRAMID
54 JUNGLE
55 ANCIENT CHINA
56 ARCHEOLOGY
57 ARCTIC & ANTARCTIC
58 BUILDING
59 PIRATE
60 NORTH AMERICAN INDIAN
61 AFRICA
62 OCEAN
63 BATTLE
64 GORILLA, MONKEY & APE
65 MEDIEVAL LIFE
66 FARM
67 SPY
68 RELIGION
69 EAGLE & BIRDS OF PREY
70 WITCHES & MAGIC-MAKERS
71 SPACE EXPLORATION
72 SHIPWRECK

PEACE MAKER
This modern painting by Liz Wright is called East Meets West. It is a version of the story of the patron saint of England, Saint George, and the Dragon. In the original story George kills the dragon, who has been devouring innocent people. In this picture the Buddha sits on the dragon's back and raises his arm to stop George. It is as if the Buddha is trying to make peace between the enemies.

Saint George raises his lance to strike the dragon.

The Buddha makes a restraining gesture toward Saint George.

SHINING LIGHT
In this modern painting from India, the Buddha is shown sitting beneath the Bodhi Tree. The halo of light around his head suggests that he has achieved enlightenment. The forefinger and thumb of his right hand touch to make the dhamma gesture—a sign that he is ready to start teaching.

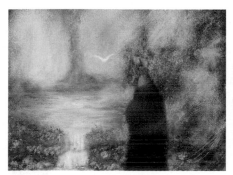

ARTIST'S IMPRESSION
Buddhism has a rich store of images that are inspiring to some modern artists. This stylized oil painting shows a Tibetan monk in his maroon robe. He is surrounded by birds, flowers, and water. This symbolizes the respect and reverence that Buddhists have for the natural world and all living things.

LIFE STORY
Little Buddha is a film by Italian director Bernardo Bertolucci. It tells the story of a group of monks who go in search of the reincarnation of a great Buddhist lama. The person they find is a small boy living in Seattle. The film also tells the life story of the Buddha himself.

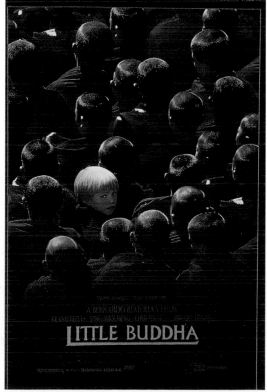

FROM BERNARDO BERTOLUCCI · CREATOR of "THE LAST EMPEROR" COMES A MAGICAL JOURNEY TO A PLACE WHERE THE PAST AND THE PRESENT MEET.

A BERNARDO BERTOLUCCI FILM

LITTLE BUDDHA

Index

Acknowledgments

Dorling Kindersley would like to thank: Birmingham Buddhist Vihara, UK, especially Venerable Dr. Rewata Dhamma and Yann Lovelock, and Karma Ling Temple, Birmingham, UK. **Special thanks also go to the models:** Yann Lovelock, Lama Rabsang, and Venerable Nagasena Bhikkhu.

All quotations used are taken from *Penguin Classics: Buddhist Scriptures*, selected and translated by Edward Conze.

The publishers would like to thank the following for their kind permission to reproduce their photographs:

a=above; b=below; c=center; l=left; r=right; t=top

Andes Press Agency: 33cr, 33br; C & D Hill 37tl; Carlos Reyes-Manzo 53br, 56bl, 59tl; **Art Directors & TRIP:** T. Bognar 22cl, 58tr; F. Good 57cr; J. Highet 18bc; T. Morse 52tl; Christopher Rennie 39br, 62bl; H. Rogers 6cr, 58tl, 63cb; J.Sweeney 29tr; B. Vikander 79cr; R. Zampese 62cl; **Ashmolean Museum:** 2br, 3bl, 26bl, 26bc, 30b, 40c; **Bridgeman Art Library, London/ New York:** British Museum 34tr; Musee Guimet, Paris 8c, 10tl, 11b, 17br, 27tr; National Museum of India, New Delhi 19br, 44r; Oriental Museum, Durham University 16c, 16tl, 17tr, 18bl, 27tl, 59br; Private Collection 24b, 41bl, 45tr, 63bl, 63t; Sarnath, Uttar Pradesh, India 20l; Victoria and Albert Museum, London 36b; **British Library:** 21tr, 24tl, 24c, 25cr, 25bl; **British**

Museum: 9b, 35c, 42tl; **Buddha Padipa Temple, Wimbledon:** 2tl, 48r; **Corbis:** Sheldan Collins 21br; Kevin Fleming 60c; Michael Freeman 51bl; Keerle Geo/Sygma 31tr; Angelo Hornak 13bl; Jeremy Horner 61t; Catherine Karnow 60br; Kurt Krieger 61bc; Liu Liqun 62r; Tim Page 53bl, 57tr; Aim Patrice/Sygma 61br; Luca I. Tettoni 16cl; Alison Wright 48tl; Michael S.Yamashita 57b, 59bl; **Ronald Grant Archive:** 63br; **Robert Harding Picture Library:** Gavin Hellier 31tl; **Hutchison Library:** Nigel Howard 53tr, 53cra, 53cr; Isabella Tree 47tl; **Icorec/Circa Photo Library:** William Holtby 56br; **Barnabas Kindersley:** 23c, 23c, 43cr, 47bl, 49tr, 49c, 51tl, 53tl; **Natural History Museum:** 19cr; **Christine Osborne:** 11tl, 18tl, 44c, 50tl, 51tc, 54cl, 59c; Nick Dawson 30tr, 40tl; Paul Gapper 47cb; **Photobank:** 58bl; **The Picture Desk:** The Art Archive: Biblioteca Nazionale Marciana,

Venice/Dagli Orti 28cl; British Museum 34l; Musee Guimet, Paris 9tr; Musee Guimet, Paris/Dagli Orti 9tl, 9cl, 57c; Navy Historical service, Vincennes, France/Dagli Orti 6tr; Private Collection, Paris/Dagli Orti 25br, 38bl; **Powell Cotton Museum:** 29br, 30tl; **Private Collection:** 28tl; **Scala Group S.P.A:** 44bl, 47tc; Museo d' Arte Orientale, Roma 6bl, 14br, 18tr, 52r; Musee Guimet 12bl; Museo Lahaur 10r; The Newark Museum/Art Resource 26tl, 32r, 37cr, 40bl, 40b, 41tr; Pierpont Morgan Library/Art Resource 41b; **Science Museum:** 24bl; **Tibet Images:** Ian Cumming 25tr; **Topham Picturepoint:** Heritage Images/British Museum: 13c, 29c, 34br, 35tr, 35br, 36tc, 42r, 54c; **Werner Forman Archive:** Christian Deydier, London 12tr; Philip Goldman Collection 32l, 33tr; Private Collection 13br; Private Collection, New York 39c.

1 BIRD
2 ROCKS & MINERALS
3 SKELETON
4 ARMS & ARMOR
5 TREE
6 POND & RIVER
7 BUTTERFLY & MOTH
8 SPORTS
9 SHELL
10 EARLY HUMANS
11 MAMMAL
12 MUSIC
13 DINOSAUR
14 PLANT
15 SEASHORE
16 FLAG
17 INSECT
18 MONEY
19 FOSSIL
20 FISH
21 CAR
22 FLYING MACHINE
23 ANCIENT EGYPT
24 ANCIENT ROME
25 CRYSTAL & GEM
26 REPTILE
27 INVENTION
28 WEATHER
29 CAT
30 BIBLE LANDS
31 EXPLORER
32 DOG
33 HORSE
34 FILM
35 COSTUME
36 BOAT
37 ANCIENT GREECE
38 VOLCANO & EARTHQUAKE
39 TRAIN
40 SHARK
41 AMPHIBIAN
42 ELEPHANT
43 KNIGHT
44 MUMMY
45 COWBOY
46 WHALE
47 AZTEC, INCA & MAYA
48 BOOK
49 CASTLE
50 VIKING
51 DESERT
52 PREHISTORIC LIFE
53 PYRAMID
54 JUNGLE
55 ANCIENT CHINA
56 ARCHEOLOGY
57 ARCTIC & ANTARCTIC
58 BUILDING
59 PIRATE
60 NORTH AMERICAN INDIAN
61 AFRICA
62 OCEAN
63 BATTLE
64 GORILLA, MONKEY & APE
65 MEDIEVAL LIFE
66 FARM
67 SPY
68 RELIGION
69 EAGLE & BIRDS OF PREY
70 WITCHES & MAGIC-MAKERS
71 SPACE EXPLORATION
72 SHIPWRECK